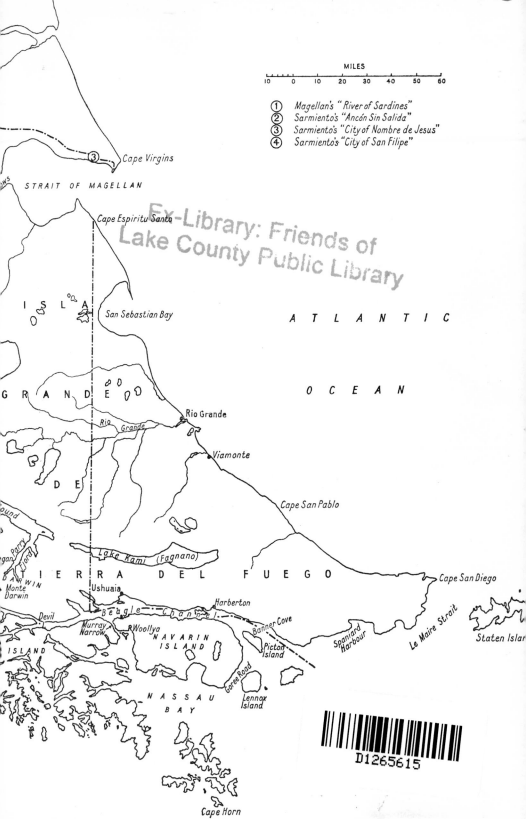

MILES

10   0   10   20   30   40   50   60

① Magellan's "River of Sardines"
② Sarmiento's "Ancón Sin Salida"
③ Sarmiento's "City of Nombre de Jesus"
④ Sarmiento's "City of San Filipe"

③ Cape Virgins

STRAIT OF MAGELLAN

Cape Espiritu Santo

ISLA

San Sebastian Bay

ATLANTIC

OCEAN

GRANDE

Rio Grande

Rio Grande

Viamonte

DE

Cape San Pablo

Lake Kami (Fagnano)

TIERRA   DEL   FUEGO

Cape San Diego

DARWIN
Monte
Darwin

Ushuaia

Parry
Fiord

Beagle Channel

Harberton

Banner Cove

Devil

Murray
Narrow

Woollya

NAVARIN
ISLAND

Picton
Island

Spaniard
Harbour

Le Maire Strait

Staten Island

ISLAND

Goree Road

Lennox
Island

NASSAU
BAY

Cape Horn

Tierra del Fuego:
the Fatal Lodestone

Tierra del Fuego: the Fatal Lodestone

ERIC SHIPTON

Charles Knight & Co. Ltd.
London & Tonbridge
1973

Charles Knight & Co. Ltd.
11-12 Bury Street, London EC3A 5AP
Dowgate Works, Douglas Road, Tonbridge
Copyright © 1973 Eric Shipton

ISBN 0 85314 194 0

Printed and bound in England by
STAPLES PRINTERS LIMITED
at The Stanhope Press, Rochester, Kent.

Contents

List of illustrations

Acknowledgments

ACKNOWLEDGMENTS are gladly made to the Nitrate Corporation of Chile for permission to reproduce plates 5 and 16; to the Società Editrice Internazionale, Turin, for plates 6 and 14, taken from Alberto M. de Agostini, *I miei viaggi nella Terra del Fuoco*, 1934; to the Royal Geographical Society for their assistance in reproducing plate 4, taken from Philip Parker King and Robert FitzRoy, *Narrative of the Surveying Voyages of H.M. Ships Adventure and Beagle*, 1830–9, and plate 10, taken from R. Cunningham, *Notes on the Natural History of the Strait of Magellan*, 1871; to the Ministry of Defence Hydrographic Department, Taunton, for plate 7; to the Mansell Collection for plate 9. Plate 8 is a portrait by Francis Lane, and is reproduced by kind permission of the Admiral President, Royal Naval College, Greenwich.

Plate 2 is an engraving by Teodoro di Bry, Frankfurt 1602; plate 3 is from Charles Darwin, *Journal of the Researches into the Natural History and Geology of the countries visited during the voyage of H.M.S. Beagle*, 1890 edition; plate 12 is from César Famin and Frédéric Lacroix, *Chile, Patagonie et îles diverses*, 1840; plate 13 is from J. Hawkesworth, *An Account of the Voyage Performed by . . . Commodore Byron, Captain Carteret, Captain Wallis and Captain Cook*, 1773; plates 11 and 15 are from the author's collection.

The tip of south America

1 The Lure

A COMBINATION of excitement and the shattering vibration of the engine made sleep impossible. At 3.30 I abandoned the attempt and climbed the ladder which led from the tiny, overcrowded cabin to the deck. The Chilean Naval Patrol Ship, *Lientur*, once an ocean-going tug, was making her way through the still water of Admiralty Sound. In the first dawn light the scene was utterly dreary. Rain fell steadily and leaden cloud hung so low that the southern shore of the channel, less than a mile away, appeared only as a thin, dark line. I shuddered and returned below to cherish my last few hours of warmth and comfort.

At seven o'clock *Lientur* swung to starboard, passed a wooded island and entered Brookes Bay. Her speed was cut to five knots and in her bows the leadsman began his rhythmic chant. Though the fjord beyond was uncharted, it was wide and open, and we had hoped to be carried many miles nearer to our goal. But the water began to shoal and presently we could see a thin line of surf stretching right across the calm surface. The reef, doubtless the terminal moraine of an ancient glacier, formed an impassable barrier. The little ship edged towards the eastern shore and dropped anchor in two fathoms. The moment of truth had arrived—disillusion or the realisation of a dream?

These channels were once inhabited by two tribes of canoe Indians, the Yahgan and the Alakaluf, now virtually extinct. When Ferdinand Magellan was groping his way through the Strait which bears his name he saw a large number of fires burning along the southern shore. They had probably been lit as rallying signals by these primitive people, who were no doubt astonished and terrified by the sudden appearance of his ships, the first they had ever seen. For this reason Magellan called his new discovery Tierra del Fuego, "Land of Fire". However misleading, the dramatic name was somehow appropriate to this savage wilderness at "the uttermost part of the earth". Magellan believed that it was part of a great southern continent, the *Terra Incognita Australis* of legend, stretching

1

away to the Antarctic. It was not until half a century later, when Drake, having passed through the Strait, was blown by north-westerly gales round Cape Horn back into the Atlantic, that it was discovered to be an island or, more correctly, an archipelago.

Much of the *Isla Grande* is gently undulating country which now supports a prosperous sheep industry. I had been there several times to visit the Bridges family in their comfortable farmstead of Viamonte on the Atlantic coast. Wandering through the silent forests or along the shore I had felt a strange sense of loneliness as though I were trespassing into a primeval world still untamed by civilised habitation. At once daunting and intensely exciting, it roused a great longing to encounter the real Fuegan wilderness and, by venturing into its yet unexplored regions, to taste the full savour of this haunting land. There was no doubt about my ultimate objective.

The highest mountains of Tierra del Fuego are in the Cordillera Darwin which occupies an uninhabited peninsula running 150 miles westward from the main island into the heart of the Horn archipelago. There the great chain of the Andes makes its final southward thrust into that notorious region of storm. Almost completely surrounded by sea, lashed by the savage gales that rage around Cape Horn, shrouded in almost perpetual mist, guarded by a massive rampart of forest which, nurtured by incessant rain, has a strangely tropical luxuriance, the range had such a reputation for inaccessibility that no one had ventured into the interior.

For me, the attraction of this hidden range was nothing new, but while for many years its influence had been confined to the imagination, physical proximity now gave it more positive form. The prospect of definite commitment added to the fascination the essential element of fear. The fact that it had repelled all would-be intruders was a measure of its formidable natural defences. What could one hope to achieve in the appalling weather said to prevail there? What would conditions be like on the high glacier passes, assuming one could get there, in the hurricanes that caused great ships to founder, in fog that persisted for weeks on end? What depth of snow-fall should be expected? Three strenuous expeditions in the mountains of Patagonia had suggested answers to some of these questions. The first two had provided some much-needed schooling in the art of survival; the third, a journey over the whole length of the Southern Ice-cap in one of the worst summers on record, had built the confidence needed to face the hazards of the Cordillera Darwin.

Two of my companions on the ice-cap, Eduardo García and

Cedomir Marangunic, had agreed to join me, together with a third Chilean mountaineer, Pancho Vivanco. After a careful study of the available charts and some air photographs we had decided to approach the range from the head of a long fjord running southward from the inlet known as Brookes Bay, on the north coast of the Peninsula. So far as we knew no one had been up this fjord, except perhaps Alakaluf canoe Indians, but it appeared to stretch far into the mountains. The Chilean Navy had undertaken to provide a ship to transport us to Brookes Bay; but as even their smallest vessel was unlikely to reach the head of the fjord, I had brought from England a large rubber boat, known as a *Zodiac*, which I had used before in Patagonia, in which to complete the journey to our base. Thus, on January 18, 1962 we had sailed from Punta Arenas in the Magellan Strait bound for one of the most exciting adventures, and certainly the least predictable, I had ever known.

While our 800 pounds of baggage was being stowed in one of the ship's boats we sipped the last of many mugs of breakfast coffee. My enthusiasm for mountain exploration had vanished, and I viewed with extreme distaste the prospect of being dumped on this uninhabited peninsula for a two-month sojourn in its vile weather. The coffee reluctantly finished, we inflated the *Zodiac*, lowered it over the side and said good-bye to our sympathetic hosts. Then, watched by the entire ship's company, I struggled for ten minutes to start the motor, until one of the officers quietly drew my attention to the fact that I had connected the petrol feed pipe the wrong way round. After this convincing display of inefficiency, we set off at high speed and overtook the boat as it was entering a small creek which we had chosen for a landing place. The baggage was taken ashore, the boat returned to be hauled aboard and presently, with a farewell toot from her siren, *Lientur* turned and gathered speed.

We stood dejectedly on the shore of the creek, closely beset by dank, dripping forest, and watched our last contact with civilised comfort disappear into the mist. The rain was still falling and already icy trickles of water had invaded my shoulders, my spine and my cringing thighs. Their woebegone faces made it clear that my companions had no more zest than I for the task in hand. How easy it had been to plan this venture in warm security at home; how easy there to set pulses racing at the mere thought of the untrodden mountains of Tierra del Fuego, to delude oneself that a single glimpse of their lonely summits would repay weeks of toil and physical misery. Now, faced with hard reality, the affair wore a very different aspect. It was not the first time that I had been prey to such feelings at the outset of a difficult enterprise; but never before had they been so poignant or so well founded. For I was well aware of the strong probability that we would achieve nothing.

One blessing relieved our gloom. There was no wind and the sea was wonderfully calm. It was still early and with a bit of luck we might reach the head of the fjord that very day. So, without even indulging in the customary brew of tea, we began packing our stores and equipment into the *Zodiac*, leaving only a small quantity of food against our return.

It was 10 o'clock when we poled the heavily laden craft out of the creek. As we started the motor, a sea-lion popped his whiskered head out of the water a few yards away, gave a hoarse, irritable grunt and disappeared. Dense masses of seaweed marked the submerged rocks of the reef and we had to be very careful to avoid getting the propeller fouled. In the open water beyond, we increased our speed to a steady four knots and braced ourselves to the prospect of a long, cold voyage.

Presently the rain stopped and the mist began to lift. The fjord was three miles across; the western shore opened to a wide gulf; at the far end of this we saw a vast glacier sweeping up from the water's edge, draped in long scarves of cloud; above it a silver gleam hinted the presence of ice peaks beyond—the corner of a veil drawn aside, a glimpse of a world aloof, ethereal, just as I had always imagined it.

Beyond the gulf, the fjord narrowed between precipitous shores. Miraculously, the weather contined to clear: a patch of blue sky, the sun, then one by one the great peaks appeared, floating high over the ragged bands of mist still clinging to the dark forested steeps above either shore. The calm surface of the channel was alive with waterfowl; they arose in their hundreds at our approach, while dolphins plunged about the *Zodiac*, their huge delight mocking our late despair.

By 2.30 we were approaching the head of the fjord and the last cloud had vanished. A sharp westward bend in the channel took us through a narrow strait into a wide lagoon set in a semi-circular wall of glaciers and mountains, 7,500 feet high. The blue water was sprinkled with blocks of floating ice carved from three massive glacier fronts; the forest on the shores between them was brilliant green in the sunlight. Rugged grandeur I had hoped to find; certainly nothing so exquisitely lovely as this.

We landed on a wooded shore and spent the rest of the afternoon, stripped to the waist under a hot sun, sorting out the food and equipment to be taken inland and stowing the boat and surplus gear in the forest. Then we pitched our camp on a grassy ledge, cooked our supper and sat gazing across the lagoon at the vast, silent amphitheatre, now a well of deepening colour.

Our task now was to find a way and carry our equipment and some six weeks' food to the interior of the range. The first problem was to penetrate the belt of dense forest which covers the outer slopes to a height of 1,500 feet above the sea and consists mostly of Antarctic beech (*nothofagus*), with heavy undergrowth between. We had expected it to be a formidable barrier which might take more than a week to surmount; but by a remarkable chance there was an easy solution close at hand. A small glacier cascading down the steep slopes above nearly reached the shore 200 yards from our landing place. The ice had shrunk leaving part of its bed exposed; a ramp of bare rock, 1,000 feet high, provided a corridor or natural staircase clean through the worst of the forest zone. This was the second example of the extraordinary luck that favoured us through-out this expedition. It was as though some benign providence were guiding our every move, dictating our every decision. We could not, it seemed, put a foot wrong.

Though the sky was still perfectly clear when we went to bed, it was raining again by dawn and the cloud hung low over the fjord. But we had seen enough to dispense with a reconnaissance and began at once back-packing our baggage up the ramp. The rock was polished smooth by ice, but it was not steep and, except for a few hundred feet in the forest above, we met with no difficulty. It took us only two days to relay all our loads over a ridge into a grassy coomb just above the tree line. The little valley was bounded on the far side by a large glacier which from this point plunged in a tangled icefall to the fjord, 1,500 feet below. The meadow where we put our second camp was saturated by the recently melted winter snow, and the summer flowers had scarcely begun to bloom.

To the south our way was barred by an unbroken wall of moun-tains which we had seen on our way up the fjord. But at the head of the glacier, hidden from the distant view, we discovered a saddle, 3,000 feet high, which led over to a level icefield, eight miles wide. It was the upper reaches of the Marinelli Glacier flowing from the highest peaks of the Cordillera Darwin to Ainsworth Bay on the north coast of the Peninsula where its huge front juts far out into the sea. It must have been regarded with wide-eyed astonishment by the early navigators of Admiralty Sound.

On January 25 we carried the last of the loads across the saddle and pitched camp at the southwest corner of the icefield. Thus, six days after landing at the head of the unknown fjord we had established ourselves in the very heart of the great range, a task which we had expected to take three times as long. Moreover, while crossing the saddle that morning we were blessed with a spell of fine weather and for two hours we had a clear view of the scores of peaks and valleys surrounding us which was invaluable for the formation of our immediate plans.

In area, the Cordillera Darwin is equivalent to the Mont Blanc, Pennine and Oberland ranges of the Alps combined, while the extent of its glaciers is far greater than those of the entire Alpine chain. To be the first to penetrate such a range, to know that every peak, every valley, every saddle is virgin ground, is a rare experience nowadays, and a thrilling situation for any mountain explorer. From an infinite number of possibilities we had already chosen three main objectives. The first was to climb the highest peak in the range. The second was to make a journey right across the Peninsula to its southern shore on the Beagle Channel; besides being the obvious way of dealing with an unexplored range, such a traverse would give the geologist, Cedomir, the best opportunity of studying its structure. The third objective, my companions' choice, was to climb a beautiful spire standing above Parry Fjord to the east, which we later named Cerro Yahgan. I would have been more than content to achieve any one of these projects; I certainly never expected to accomplish all three.

When FitzRoy was exploring the Beagle Channel, he named one of the peaks above the northern shore "Mount Darwin" after the young scientist who was with him at the time. It is not known for certain which peak he chose and as the name has since been given to the whole range and the highest peak was still un-named we decided to call it Monte Darwin. We had not yet identified our mountain, but we guessed that it must be one of a group of peaks around a high coomb to the south of our camp. The only direct route to it was up an icefall, some 2,000 feet high, which looked so formidable that we had no hesitation in rejecting it. We decided instead to make a detour up a big tributary glacier to the west in the hope of finding from that direction both an easier approach to the coomb and a way across the Range.

The brief interlude of clear weather which greeted our arrival on the Marinelli icefield had broken by the time we had pitched camp, and the storm which then began lasted for more than a week. Hitherto we had been largely protected from the wind by the

mountains encircling the head of the fjord; now we were exposed
to its full force. But we were snug inside our double-skinned Antarctic
Pyramid tent, and the fact that it had survived the worst that the
weather on the Patagonian ice-cap could throw at us inspired a
pleasant sense of security. Indeed, provided it was properly pitched
with plenty of snow piled on its wide skirts or snow-flaps, it was
virtually indestructible.

A novel item of equipment (novel for me that is) that I had
brought from England was a small radio transmitter supplied by the
Royal Navy and designed for sea rescue. It weighed 20 pounds; the
power was generated by means of a crank handle, and it had a
12 foot telescopic aerial mast. It had been arranged that we should
communicate with the Chilean naval station on Dawson Island,
south of Punta Arenas, while we were at our landing place; thereafter they were to listen for us at 5.30 each evening until our return
in case we got into trouble and needed help. However, we failed
to make ourselves heard from the shore of the fjord, though Dawson
Island was well within the theoretical range of our instrument,
presumably because of the mountains surrounding us. So, reluctantly,
we had carried the wretched thing with us, hoping to achieve better
results from a higher altitude; but even at 3,000 feet, though we
could hear their signals quite clearly, they still failed to receive ours,
and we decided to leave the radio at our main depot on the Marinelli
icefield.

Experience in Patagonia had taught us that it was useless to wait
for the weather and that, however severe the conditions, we must
attempt to make some progress each day. So every morning we
turned out and groped our way back and forth in mist and blinding
drift, reconnoitring one landmark after another and relaying loads
in short stages. It was slow and exacting work. For the most part
we were working through another ice-fall, which would normally
have been quite easy; but in these conditions each movement had
to be made with extreme deliberation. In the first place it was vital
that we never lost our sense of position and direction, for our tracks
were generally obliterated within a few minutes. Luckily, Cedomir
had a superb feeling for topography and he was never at fault. As
a rule visibility was restricted to a few yards which made it very
difficult to detect crevasses or to discover in which direction they
ran, and we often had a nasty feeling that we were all on the same
crevasse at the same time. In fact, during this period, we only sustained one fall into a crevasse, and the victim, Eduardo, was
extracted unharmed. Most of the time we wore skis which was a

partial protection so long as we were moving in a direction across the line of the crevasses.

We had, of course, to be extremely careful in siting our supply dumps. To be sure of finding them we always put them near at least three recognisable objects, such as a rock outcrop or the end of a crevasse, so that, by taking compass bearings to each, we could locate the exact spot even when the dump was buried in drift snow. To make doubly sure, Cedomir and I took independent sets of bearings.

Even on the worst days the mist would lift occasionally, giving us fleeting glimpses of some part of our immediate surroundings; gradually their various features became familiar and were fitted in to our remembered picture of the whole. But they would have meant little had it not been for the lucky chance of those few hours of fine weather at the start; without it the whole of that week would certainly have been wasted. As it was, we had a positive intermediate objective—a spur between the western glacier and another joining it from the south, where we established a well-stocked advance base.

From there we struck south and after two days of strenuous climbing on steep, wind-polished ice we reached the crest of a ridge, 8,000 feet high. It was 5.30 on February 2: at that very moment, for the first time in nine days, the encircling fog vanished and we were bathed in the evening sunshine with a clear sky above. The timing of the transformation could hardly have been more dramatic. We were standing at one end of a crescent wall like a large atoll in a sea of cloud. In the central "lagoon" lay the coomb we had seen from the Marinelli Glacier; across it, at the opposite end of the crescent, stood the highest peak of the range, our Monte Darwin, its summit less than 1,000 feet above us.

The ridge was crowned by a massive plume of ice and our tent was placed beneath its crest which curved overhead like a breaking wave. Though tired and hungry, we spent the long hours of golden twilight climbing a small peak on the rim of the crescent wall, there to catch first sight, far away to the south, of the islands— Londonderry, Gordon, Stewart—of the Horn Archipelago. Night fell in unwonted calm, and because we were tired we failed to stow our belongings with proper care. Soon after midnight we were smitten by a mighty storm, and in spite of the snug position of the camp, one of our food bags was swept away and lost.

Late the next morning we packed up amid swirling drift and plunged into the cloud-filled valley beneath. There, at the western foot of Monte Darwin, completely protected from the wind, we pitched camp and, reducing our rations by one-third, settled in for a long siege. It was a strange place, that silent coomb, enfolded by the crescent wall, a bowl of tranquillity at the heart of the tempestuous land we had come to woo. Already our patient, groping struggles had yielded the key to its inner sanctuary, and we began to realise that we were to be counted among its more favoured votaries.

The more hostile the natural environment the more important is the element of luck. It is not surprising therefore that this has played a very large part in the stories of pioneer travel in Tierra del Fuego, whose reputation for foul weather is unsurpassed. Always the odds on failure have been heavily stacked, and success won only on a slender margin of chance. Magellan might never have made his great discovery but for the sudden easterly gale which drove his ships, out of control, through the First and Second Narrow; and no doubt a dozen times through the weeks which followed he came nearer to disaster than he knew. If the fantastic storm which swept Drake eastward around Cape Horn had started a few days earlier while he was still in the Strait, his *Golden Hind* might well have been destroyed and several chapters of history left unwritten. But in these tales of survival and calamity there can be seen another factor, almost as important though less easy to define. It seems to lie in a philosophical attitude: an ability to understand, to come to terms with and to accept the environment, which some men have acquired and others fatally lacked.

The conditions we met with in the Cordillera Darwin were neither exceptionally good nor unusually bad. Our good luck lay in the timing of the weather changes in relation to our movements: however severe the intervening storms, clear spells always occurred when they were most needed. There is no doubt, however, that we would have been unable to profit from this happy circumstance had it not been for several lessons we had learnt in Patagonia, lessons which many years of mountain exploration in other parts of the world had not taught me. One of these was the urgent need for action even on the worst days, not only for the sake of morale—though this was always an important consideration—but because even the blindest reconnaissance provided useful contact with our surroundings and a few seconds' vision could furnish a vital clue. Often we looked back at chances which would have been missed if we had yielded to the temptation of going to ground to ride out a particularly bad storm. But though we may claim to have had some hand in the shaping of our fortunes, I have often wondered, not without a slight inward shudder, how we would have fared in some of the more extravagant excesses of Fuegan weather.

On the day after our arrival in the Silent Coomb, we made a thorough reconnaissance of our mountain, now standing some 3,000 feet above us, and cut steps up the lower slopes. So when, characteristically, the next morning dawned fine, we were able to seize our advantage without a moment's delay. At 9 o'clock we stood for the first time at the highest point of the great white range which, through the centuries, has formed the elusive backcloth to so many dramatic events. It had been an exciting race which we won with only a few minutes to spare before the mountain was once more wrapped in cloud. That evening we celebrated success by resuming our full ration of food; and after supper we lay listening to the gale once more booming on the heights above.

Before leaving the Coomb we climbed a peak on the southern part of the crescent wall. As the wind was in the southwest, we remained in comparative shelter until we reached the crest of the wall a few hundred feet below the summit, where we were met by a savage blast. Unable to stand we had to crawl forward on hands and knees, digging the picks of our ice-axes into the wind-packed snow. At one point a large chunk of granite hurtled past Cedomir's head and buried itself in the ridge a feet beyond. We could not tell where it came from for we were then near the summit of the peak and there was no rock outcrop anywhere in the vicinity. The wind was so warm that it melted the drift as it was whipped from the surface and in a few minutes we were soaked to the skin as though we had been standing before a powerful hose.

The operation was well worth while: for a short time we had a comprehensive view of the southern side of the range which was vital for the achievement of our next project, a journey over to the Beagle Channel. Even so it was by no means easy to find a route, and as we groped our way on compass bearings from point to point I was again more than thankful for Cedomir's extraordinary sense of direction and his skill in recognising minor topographical features. Luckily, too, the wind during the next few days was not severe and we had several brief spells of clear weather. When these occurred, usually in the evening or early morning, our sombre monochrome world became suffused with the colour, delicate as egg-shell porcelain, which is characteristic of those southern latitudes.

One evening we reached the edge of a glacier plateau and descended beneath the cloud level to a high spur running southward between two inlets of the Beagle Channel, 4,000 feet below. From there we gazed eastward to Devil Island, where one of FitzRoy's men had been scared by an inquisitive owl into the conviction that he had seen a satanic vision. Beyond it we could just discern Murray Narrow leading to Woollya and Jemmy Button's country. The islands of the westward passage, etched in phantom light beneath a dark pall, looked wild and very remote.

The next morning, leaving the tent standing, we set out unencumbered with loads. A swift glissade down a wide snow gully took us below the cloud ceiling which had descended during the night. A further scramble down a series of cliffs brought us into a wide amphitheatre of gently sloping meadows where we waded knee-deep through drifts of white and yellow flowers. The air was heavy with their scent. The encircling precipice topped with cloud, isolated us from our frozen world above, and the sudden contrast enhanced the beauty of the place. It looked so warm and friendly, so eminently habitable, that it was strange to think that we were probably the first human beings to reach it; for the canoe Indians who used to inhabit the Beagle Channel never strayed far inland.

Even unladen, the penetration of the forest belt to the shore was a hard struggle, and the return was even worse. Indeed we badly misjudged the time and we were lucky to find our way back to camp when it was almost too dark to see. The point was emphasised a few hours later by the onset of another storm. For once we decided to have a day of rest.

That storm heralded the start of the worst spell of weather we encountered during the whole expedition. A series of violent gales interspersed with exceptionally heavy snowfall made progress very slow and laborious, and we began to doubt our ability to recross the range before our supply of food was exhausted. As a precaution we again reduced our daily ration. A food dump which we had left on the way over was buried under six feet of fresh snow, and although we located its position within a few yards, we had to dig and probe for two hours before finding the tip of an upright ski which had been placed to mark the spot. When eventually we reached our main depot at the head of the Marinelli Glacier it was similarly buried, and we certainly would not have found it but for the fact that the top of the 12-foot aerial mast was projecting from the surface of the snow. For the depot had been carelessly sited on a flat expanse, too far from any land mark to get an accurate compass fix. In fact the loss of the dump would not have been fatal, as by then we were only a couple of days away from our shore base;

but it would have meant our abandoning any further operations.

As it was, we had a week left before we must start back to keep our rendezvous in Brookes Bay. If our luck held there might be enough time to tackle our third and final objective, the ascent of the beautiful peak of Cerro Yahgan. Using our skis as a sledge, we made a long haul across the Marinelli Basin and then climbed an icefall to the foot of one of the granite buttresses of the mountain where, late in the evening, we pitched our tent in a snow hollow. Though the worst of the storm had subsided, the weather was far from promising, but we hoped the next day to carry the camp a thousand feet higher.

I was in the habit of waking before dawn, and when the next morning I opened my eyes to find it quite light inside the double-skinned tent, I thought that I had overslept. Then, finding it was still only 2.45, I scrambled up and thrust my head through the sleeve entrance. It was uncanny! I could hardly believe that it had happened yet again. The moon, a little past full, was riding in a cloudless sky; absolute stillness filled our shining hollow. I roused my companions and after a hurried breakfast we started.

For once it was freezing hard and on the crusted snow we climbed swiftly to meet the dawn. Around us the peaks stood like sheeted spectres; behind, sixty miles away, the slender spire of Monte Sarmiento, beacon of the early navigators, pierced the dark blue shadows of the western sky. A thousand feet up we were faced by a series of huge crevasses backed by vertical or overhanging walls. Each in turn looked impassable; but each time the lucky chance of a slender snow bridge and a crack in the wall behind enabled us to overcome the obstacle. The last of the walls, barely 100 feet high, took an hour and a half to surmount, while I fretted, unable to believe that the miraculous weather would hold. Beyond was a steep ridge of hard ice, and from its narrow crest we looked straight down 7,000 feet to Parry Fjord, a silver ribbon between its dark green shores. The ridge was capped by a cornice which girdled the apex of the peak like a gigantic crystal mushroom. But a narrow corridor gave passage beneath it until we found a break in the overhanging ice; and at 12.30 we scrambled through to the summit. The issue had remained in doubt until the last moment, and once again we were only just in time to beat the cloud.

There was still no wind and we could afford to take our time on the descent, and relish the sense of relaxation following the urgency of the past nine hours. I was tired when we got back to camp, but very happy and looking forward to a long lie-in the next morning.

Around midnight I was wakened by a storm of unusual violence which continued to mount through the early hours in a shattering crescendo, until we could not hear each other's shouts above the roar of the wind and the tearing sound caused by particles of drift hurled against the tent canvas. At 4.30 the tent collapsed over our heads. I thought that the indestructible Pyramid had at last met its match and that two of the poles had snapped; but we discovered later that one of its sides had been driven four feet into the hard-packed snow beneath, and that the tent itself was intact.

By then it was light and in the pandemonium of madly flapping canvas we managed to find and put on our boots and windproofs and to pack most of our belongings. Then I crawled outside, stood up and was instantly blown flat on my face, while my balaclava was whipped from my head and vanished over the rim of the ice-fall. Our activities during the next two hours must have looked like one of those slap-stick comedies of the old silent films. Again and again we were hurled to the ground when we tried to stand, and we had to crawl around on hands and knees struggling to dismantle the tent and at the same time prevent it from being torn from our grasp. The task was further complicated by the fact that it was impossible to face the drift-laden wind. Cedomir's pack weighing some fifty pounds, was swept into a crevasse 200 yards away; luckily it lodged on a ledge only twenty feet down and was recovered. When at length we had salvaged the tent and tied it in a rough bundle, we dragged everything down into the ice-fall where we found some shelter. Resting for a while, we watched dense masses of snow hurled across the cliffs and corries of Cerro Yahgan with a noise like the thunder of a major ice avalanche. Had we been on the mountain in those conditions we would not have survived. I have only experienced two other wind-storms of comparable ferocity; both were in Patagonia.

Now, beyond our wildest expectations, we had accomplished all three of our main objectives, and although we still had several days in hand we were disposed to turn homewards and spend them in gentler pleasures. The storm continued, but by the time we had reached the Marinelli basin it had lost some of its deadly malice, and the very next day, by dint of hard marching, we reached the alp where we had placed our second camp six weeks before. The flower-strewn meadows, the tracery of green foliage framing the glacier walls of the cirque, the deep forest plunging to the lagoon— it was a beautiful spot; to us then, our starved senses feasting on the colours, the smells and the sounds of the living world, it was enchanting. There was something very special, too, about going down to the fjord: the smell of the tidal shore and the cry of sea birds, themselves always exciting, were deliciously unfamiliar in the context of a mountain expedition.

When we reached the shore where we had left the *Zodiac* hidden in the forest, nearly a week still remained before we were due to be picked up at Brookes Bay by the Chilean Navy. So we cruised down the fjord in easy stages, while Cedomir examined its geology and I made a collection of *collembola* and other small creatures requested by the British Museum. But our time was mostly devoted to sheer self-indulgence. Choosing the most attractive creeks and bays for our camp sites, we fished for star-crabs (*sentoya*) from amongst the forest of kelp in the deep pools at low tide, and even dived into the icy water from sheer bravado; we ate enormous quantities of mussels and sea-urchins, our relish for fresh food offsetting the lack of condiments. Best of all were the hours spent beside great log fires, the lapping of the tide and the shifting lights of the fjord mingling with our dreams.

This was just how early navigators had sometimes found these strange Fuegan channels; it was one aspect of the scene which had become so poignantly familiar to Peter Carder and Sarmiento, to FitzRoy and Skyring; it explained the many references to benevolence and gentle beauty among the horrific tales of hardship in a cruel and hostile land. Here, amidst all this bounty, it was hard to understand why so many of the castaways had died of hunger; here the stories of survival seemed less incredible. But we needed no reminding that this was only one side of the coin.

Gradually the great mountains receded into the background where they had always belonged. But they were as much part of the Fuegan scene as the channels, the forests or the storm-lashed coasts, and knowing them as no one had known them before, far from diminishing their appeal, deepened our awareness of the whole. In the striving for our objectives as much as in their accomplishment, we had won a sense both of intimacy with this wild land and of kinship, however humble and remote, with our fellow pioneers through the centuries.

2 Magellan reaches the Pacific

THE first voyage around the world was the climax of three decades of geographical discovery never rivalled before or since. It was one of the great milestones of human history, if only because it demonstrated to the ordinary man the incredible fact—hitherto the mere conjecture of learned philosophers—that he was living on a globe.

Contemporary writers tell us little about the character of Ferdinand Magellan, the man responsible for this prodigious achievement, and the personality behind the austere, monkish figure shown in several of his portraits remains tantalisingly obscure. From the conduct of his famous voyage it is obvious that he had extraordinary courage, acute intelligence and inflexible determination. Apart from these qualities it seems that he was a man of small stature, deep religious conviction, strong family ties and staunch loyalty both to his friends and to the subordinates he trusted. Of the whole period of his life prior to the voyage (some thirty-nine years) very little is known, and his many biographers have been obliged to build their accounts of it largely upon conjecture drawn from very slender evidence. It is not surprising, therefore, that they should differ widely on many crucial issues. Happily, the main events of the voyage itself were more fully recorded. This was largely due to the fact that a young Italian named Antonio Pigafetta, "desirous of seeing the wonderful things of the ocean", joined the fleet and, sailing for the most part in Magellan's flagship, kept a lucid diary of his three years' odyssey. One of the few survivors, he published this journal shortly after his return.

Magellan was born about 1480 into a junior branch of a noble family living in North Portugal. At the age of twelve he became a page at the court of King John II in Lisbon. Though this may seem poor preparation for a future explorer, it probably provided him with valuable training, for the royal pages were subjected to stern discipline, and besides their court duties they were intensively schooled in the arts of horsemanship and armed combat. They were also required to study cartography, and celestial navigation; and

15

in Lisbon at that time there was no lack of able instructors in these subjects. Later, it seems that he was employed as a clerk in the maritime department of India House.

Young Ferdinand certainly grew up in stirring times. The voyage of Diaz around the Cape of Good Hope may have made no great impression on a child of seven living in a remote country house; but for a lad of thirteen, at the very heart of the maritime world, the impact of Columbus' discovery of a new continent across the Atlantic must have been profound, opening as it did vistas of fabulous adventure. No doubt it lent cogency to his studies and may well have initiated his lifelong devotion to astronomy.

It is hard, even in our own age of rapid change, to appreciate the ferment of excitement caused by this explosion of geographical discovery, this sudden, seemingly limitless, expansion of the accessible world. Almost every year expeditions returned with tales of new and wondrous lands beyond the sea. Though the losses in men and ships were great, the financial gains were often enormous. Moreover, unlike today, almost every able bodied man was eligible to take part in the epic adventures.

For Portugal, by far the most important of these voyages were those of Vasco da Gama. In 1497, he sailed from Lisbon with four ships to exploit Diaz's discovery of ten years before, and returned two years later having reached India. The significance of this achievement was that it gave Portugal direct access to the riches of the east, a trade which had hitherto been the monopoly of Arab and Venetian merchants. Moreover, since the Treaty of Tordesillas (1494) had, by Papal decree, given her the sole right to all newly discovered lands east of the 40th meridian W. (which bisects the North Atlantic) it opened an immense new field for Portuguese imperial expansion, perhaps even embracing the legendary Spice Islands themselves. On his second expedition, which left Lisbon in 1502 with twenty ships, da Gama established a foothold on the west coast of India.

Why, during this period of intense activity, Magellan remained so long in Lisbon is something of a mystery. He was already well into his twenties, an age when many of his privileged class had travelled far along the road to high distinction, and when most of his seafaring contemporaries had already had many years of practical experience. To account for this curious circumstance it has been suggested that, while at court, he had somehow incurred the enmity of King Manuel, who had succeeded John in 1495, and who refused to allow him to join in any of the overseas ventures. Certainly his later treatment by the King lends colour to this theory. Whatever the truth of the matter, it was not until 1505, when he must have been about twenty-five, that he set out on his first maritime adventure.

In March of that year a fleet of twenty-five ships sailed under the command of Francisco de Almeida with the object of seizing naval control of the Indian Ocean and consolidating Portugal's trading position in Asia. Almeida's instructions were to acquire, either by conquest or by treaty with local potentates, a series of bases at key points along the east coast of Africa and the west coast of India, and then to establish himself as Viceroy of the whole region. Magellan joined the fleet, apparently without rank, together with his cousin and close friend, Francisco Serrano.

Magellan served for seven years in the east, playing a minor role in one of the most dramatic episodes in the history of European imperial expansion. From occasional references to him by contemporary writers it is possible to get some idea of his activities. For two years he was closely involved in the arduous campaign to capture and hold strategic points along the East African coast, and some of his exploits received special mention in the reports sent back to Lisbon. During much of this time he served under Nuño Vaz Pereira, one of the ablest captains in the fleet and, later, its second-in-command, by whom he seems to have been highly regarded. This might have led to his early promotion, but unfortunately, early in 1509, Pereira was killed in the fleet action off Diu, which resulted in the virtual destruction of Arab naval power in the Indian Ocean. Fighting beside his captain, Magellan himself was severely wounded.

Soon after this, Almeida was replaced by Alfonso d'Albuquerque in circumstances of considerable mutual animosity. There is reason to believe that, by his loyalty to his former chief, Magellan incurred the displeasure of the new Viceroy and that this had an important bearing upon his subsequent misfortunes.

After the Battle of Diu the Portuguese hold on the Indian coast seemed to be sufficiently secure to warrant further eastward expansion, and in August 1509, a small fleet was despatched to Malacca. Its object was to establish direct trade with that city, which owed its supreme importance as a commercial centre to its position in the gateway to the Far East. The attempt was foiled by the duplicity of the Sultan who was no doubt well aware of the Portuguese methods of conquest, and the fleet barely escaped annihilation. We know that Magellan took part in the expedition because of two acts of great heroism which he performed; one of these was concerned with the rescue of his friend Serrano from a seemingly hopeless situation. We are also told of another occasion when, shipwrecked on an uninhabited island, he behaved with great unselfishness and concern for his comrades.

In those harsh days, such citations for gallantry were not lightly accorded to obscure individuals, and we may infer from these brief glimpses that he served with considerable zeal. But though he was getting plenty of adventure, there is nothing to show how he gained the skill and experience which were to make him one of the greatest navigators of all time.

When in June 1511, a second expedition of nineteen ships was sent to Malacca, it seems that Magellan and Serrano were each given command of a caravel. This time the object was to capture the city by force of arms and, after a very hard struggle, this was accomplished. It was perhaps Albuquerque's most striking achievement and certainly his most profitable; for the value of the booty was enormous. Moreover, having gained control of the Strait of Malacca, the way was now wide open to the unknown seas beyond, above all to the Moluccas, the Spice Islands, the very source of the most coveted treasures of the East. As soon as he had established his position, the Viceroy despatched Antonio d'Abreu with three ships to find the fabled archipelago.

Here is one of the most teasing enigmas of Magellan's career. Did he take any part whatever in this expedition? We know that Abreu commanded one of the three ships and that Francisco Serrano commanded another. One contemporary historian asserts that Magellan commanded the third, while others are equally emphatic that he did not. Another theory, equally unsupported by solid evidence, is that about this time he took his caravel on a lone and unauthorised voyage northeastwards across the China Sea to discover the archipelago now known as the Philippine Islands. If, as the weight of evidence seems to suggest, he took no part in either of these ventures, one wonders when he can have won the reputation as a navigator and explorer that he must have acquired before the start of his great enterprise; for, by June the following year (1512), he was back in Lisbon.

Meanwhile, Serrano was engaged in a romantic exploit which was to have some bearing on Magellan's career. The little fleet reached Amboina in the Moluccas where it took on a cargo of spices. Early on the return voyage Serrano's vessel became detached from the others and, after a series of fantastic adventures, which included the loss of their ship and the timely capture of a Chinese junk, he and his crew reached Ternate (N.W. of New Guinea). There, by helping the ruler to defeat his enemies and other adroit manoevres, Serrano won a position of considerable power in the Spice Islands, which he continued to enjoy until his death eight years later. Somehow he managed to send letters to Magellan giving him information about the geography of the region and urging him to come and help him to exploit his unique situation. That Magellan had every intention of doing so is evident from one of the letters he sent to his cousin and which has survived.

On his return to Lisbon, now a hive of commercial activity and bloated with the riches of the Orient, Magellan might reasonably have expected some substantial reward for seven years of arduous and distinguished service; but whether because of his impolitic loyalty to the former Viceroy or the King's personal animosity, he received none. In August 1513, he joined a massive punitive expedition against the Moors in Morocco where he served as a soldier, a strange role for a former sea captain. If his motive were to win favour he was again disappointed, for he returned after a year's campaigning with nothing to show for it but a wounded knee which left him with a limp for the rest of his life.

Shortly after his return from Morocco, Magellan, at a public audience, asked the king for another appointment in the Navy. This apparently reasonable request was met with a snub so cruelly humiliating that the wretched man was left with no alternative but to retire into obscurity and abandon all hope of professional advancement in his own country. There is no reason to suppose that he had made any specific proposal, so that in this important respect his rejection is hardly comparable with that of Columbus some twenty years before.

Magellan was by no means the only recipient of shabby treatment at the hands of King Manuel. The brilliant achievements of Vasco da Gama and Francisco de Almeida had been meanly rewarded, and scores of others, humbler perhaps but equally deserving the gratitude of their monarch, failed to get their deserts. Many, through bitterness or poverty, had left the country to seek their fortunes in Spain where some had already attained distinction. It is surprising that Magellan did not immediately follow their example. In fact he remained in Portugal for another three years.

It is reasonable to suppose that it was soon after his humiliation that he began seriously to consider trying to find a westward route to the Spice Islands. A phrase used in his letter to Serrano—that he would come to him "if not by Portugal, then by way of Spain"—

is suggestive of this. The idea must have occurred to him before, for it had been discussed in maritime circles ever since men began to suspect that the land discovered by Columbus was not part of Asia (as the great navigator continued to believe to his dying day). But as the opening of a way to the Orient through the Spanish hemisphere would be against the interests of Portugal, Magellan is not likely to have proposed the project while seeking employment under King Manuel.

Magellan's activities during those three years are, like most of his life, cloaked in mystery, and the only fact that we know for certain is that he formed a close association with Ruy Faleiro which developed into a partnership in the planning of his great enterprise. As one of the foremost cosmographers of his time, Faleiro had much to teach him about two of his main problems: the determination of longitude and the probable size of the globe. A further bond between the two men was the fact that the astronomer had also fallen from royal favour (probably on account of his irascible temper) and intended to emigrate to Spain. This friendship between the practical seaman and the brilliant scientific theorist suggests a plausible reason why Magellan delayed his departure for so long. Ever since the time of Henry the Navigator, Portugal had been the hub of the maritime world. Nowhere else was there such a wealth of knowledge about distant seas and shores, nowhere such a number of sailors who had taken part in their discovery. It seems unlikely, as some historians claim, that at this time Magellan had direct access to the marine archives in Lisbon, but there were other means by which he could have obtained the information he needed. He must, for example, have been acquainted with many of the men who had sailed along the coast of South America with Coelho, Jaques or John of Lisbon, during the past fifteen years and who would recount their experiences and discoveries. For although he was despised in court circles he must surely have found sympathy among his less sophisticated and perhaps disenchanted fellow sailors. However this may be, when he finally left his native land his plans were well matured.

His arrival at Seville in October 1517, marked the beginning of a bewildering transformation of his fortunes. Hitherto an obscure nonentity, a one-time sea captain deprived of his command, a social outcast, we find him here the honoured guest of a man of high degree who was willing and able to promote his welfare and to afford him access to the most exalted potentates in the land. It is hard to account for this cordial reception unless there had been

prior negotiations and unless Magellan had considerably more to
offer in the way of experience than is generally admitted. Certainly
at that time Portuguese navigators were much in demand in Spain;
but many distinguished sailors had already come over—for example
Francisco Serrano's brother John—without being accorded such an
open-handed welcome.

His host in Seville was Diogo Barbosa, a Commander of the
Order of Santiago and the controller of the Arsenal. Though
himself a Portuguese emigré he had lived in Spain for fourteen years
and was now a man of considerable importance. His son, Duarte,
who had recently completed a massive work on the geography of
Asia, had served in India under Almeida at the same time as
Magellan. It is not improbable that the two young men had met
and maintained contact, and that the Barbosas were already aware
of Magellan's plans. The fact that Duarte himself took part in the
great enterprise lends some colour to this theory. But whatever the
antecedents of Magellan's friendship with the Barbosas, there can
be little doubt of its warmth. Within two months of his arrival in
Seville he had married Diogo's daughter, Beatriz. Considering her
father's wealth and rank, his ready consent to the union was surely
a singular mark of esteem.

Under this genial patronage Magellan's plans prospered with
almost incredible alacrity, particularly considering the turbulent
state of Spanish politics at that time. His cause was espoused by a
senior official of the Casa de Contratacion (India Office) who acted
with such despatch that by the end of February 1518, only four
months after his arrival, his project received Royal assent. To achieve
this he had first to convince the council of ministers of its validity.
At this crucial interview he was supported by Faleiro, who produced
evidence for a seductive theory that the Spice Islands, with their
enormous potential wealth, were actually within the Spanish
hemisphere. It is less easy to understand how Magellan managed to
persuade the council that a westward passage to the Orient really
existed. Certainly the arguments he used must have been shrewdly
presented to win the confidence of hard-headed inquisitors who can
have had no predisposition in his favour.

Whatever qualities his biographers have bestowed upon Magellan,
charm is not among them; and yet the extraordinary successes—
social, professional and romantic—which marked his first few
months in Spain surely suggest something closely akin. His most
significant conquest was with King Charles V himself. The eighteen-
year-old monarch had only arrived in the country in the previous

September, and his throne was far from secure, but in spite of his manifold problems he evidently formed such a high opinion of the little Portuguese navigator that he took a deep interest in the expedition and offered his personal intervention should difficulties arise in the course of its preparation. As further proof of his confidence he awarded Magellan the title of Commander of the Order of Santiago.

He was soon to have urgent need of this royal favour. Not surprisingly, when King Manuel heard of the proposed expedition, he was furious and made strong diplomatic representations to have it quashed. These were politely but firmly rejected. He also instructed his ambassador to induce Magellan, with promises of rich reward, to return to Portugal, and when this manoevre failed he ordered his agents in Seville to do all they could to sabotage the preparations. But there was still more sinister influence at work. Bishop Fonseca of Burgos was President of the Casa de Contratacion, and thus virtually the head of maritime affairs in the country. Though a strong supporter of the expedition, his motives were far from disinterested, for he had every intention of securing a major share of the profits which might result from its success. With this in view he arranged for the appointment of his nephew (some say his natural son), Juan de Cartagena, as second-in-command. Between them and two other Spanish captains, Quesada and Mendoza, it was planned that Magellan should be deposed and, if necessary, murdered at a suitable stage of the voyage, presumably when the westward passage had been discovered and he had become expendable. Even if others were not implicated in the plot at its inception, they were certainly recruited at a later date. Magellan may well have suspected the treachery, but there was nothing he could do about it in view of the exalted position of its author. He did, however, forestall an attempt by Fonseca to place Cartagena on an equal footing with himself.

The expedition was financed partly from the Royal Treasury and partly by Christopher de Haro, an international banker with vast financial interests in the East and West Indian trades. It consisted of five ships: *Trinidad*, 110 tons, Magellan's flagship; *San Antonio*, 120 tons, *Concepcion*, 90 tons, and *Victoria*, 85 tons, commanded respectively by the three Spanish captains, Cartagena, Gaspar Quesada and Luis de Mendoza; and, lastly, *Santiago*, 75 tons, captained by Magellan's cousin, John Serrano. The total complement of officers and crew was about 270, composed of men of many different nationalities including one, a master gunner, from

England. After endless delays the fleet finally sailed from Santa Lucar at the mouth of the Guadalquivir on September 20, 1519. A week later it reached Tenerife.

There Magellan received a letter from his father-in-law, despatched by a fast caravel shortly after his departure, warning him of the plot to seize control of the expedition. It was not long before he had tangible evidence of the menace. Soon after leaving Tenerife, Juan de Cartagena began a campaign of insubordination and calculated insult evidently designed to sap the authority of the Captain-General and provoke a quarrel. For some time Magellan held his hand, and his apparent meekness encouraged Cartagena to become more and more aggressive, until one day when the captains were assembled for a conference in the flagship, the Spaniard was seized and put in irons. Though he shouted to his compatriots for help, Magellan's mastery of the situation was so complete that none of them stirred to his defence. Nevertheless this demonstration of disloyalty and the knowledge that it was harboured by others among his senior officers must have been an appalling burden to bear through the anxious months ahead.

On leaving Tenerife, instead of setting a course to the westward of the Cape Verde Islands laid down in his stated plan, Magellan steered southward along the African coast. There is little doubt that this change was due to his knowledge that several Portuguese squadrons had been sent to intercept him and his determination to avoid them. Nevertheless, it caused him to run into serious difficulties which, since he was not willing to divulge his reasons, weakened his prestige and strengthened the hands of his enemies. For three weeks the ships were becalmed under a scorching tropical sun near the Gulf of Guinea; for nearly a month after that they were buffeted by heavy storms and headwinds. As a result of these delays, rations of food and water had to be reduced, and it was not until December 13, that the fleet dropped anchor in Santa Lucia Bay.

This beautiful harbour, the site of the modern city of Rio de Janeiro, must have seemed like paradise to the sailors after more than ten weeks continuously at sea. The local inhabitants were friendly and so eager for barter that they were willing to offer their children in exchange for such treasures as knives and mirrors, while the young women were by no means reluctant to disperse their favours. There was, too, a great abundance of fresh meat, vegetables and delicious tropical fruit to delight the palates of men long weary of a diet of salt pork and ship's biscuit. For a bare fortnight they stayed in this delectable spot and on December 26 they resumed their southward voyage. Had they realised the appalling hardship and privation, the unrelieved suffering that was to be their lot during the coming year, one wonders if any, if Magellan himself, would have had the courage to face the ordeal.

Of all the unanswered questions surrounding Magellan's life, the most intriguing is this. Did he *know* of the existence of a passage westward from the Atlantic into another ocean beyond; had he any substantial evidence of the whereabouts of such a passage; or was his great enterprise based on nothing but pure conjecture, upon the belief, perhaps, that the American land-mass might terminate southward in the same fashion as the African? Before considering this question it should be remembered that the belief in the existence of a great ocean washing both the eastern shores of Asia and the western shores of America was in itself sheer speculation. Crossing the isthmus of Darien (Panama) in 1513, Balboa had seen a body of water which he called the "South Sea"; it was also known that there was a large expanse of open sea lying to the east of Cathay and the Spice Islands; but that the two were parts of the same ocean there was no evidence whatever.

Of the many Portuguese voyages during the first decade of the 16th century, two are of special interest in this context. Both were privately sponsored expeditions, one in 1501 commanded by Gonzalo Coelho, the other in 1503 by Christopher Jaques. Apparently both sailed far southward along the coast of South America and one may even have reached beyond latitude 50°S. Surprisingly little is known about either, and it has been suggested that King Manuel impounded their charts and suppressed all information about their discoveries. Assuming that these related to a possible westward passage, his motives for such an action are clear enough. Nevertheless, Magellan, who was then in Lisbon, may well have received first-hand accounts of the voyages. It is perhaps a significant circumstance that the sponsor of both was Christopher de Haro who had a large stake in Magellan's expedition.

In 1515 and again in 1520, Johan Schoner, Professor of Mathematics in Nuremberg, constructed a globe on which the South American Continent was depicted as terminating in a point and separated by a narrow strait from another land-mass to the south. This representation was apparently based upon a somewhat garbled account, published in German a short time before, of a Portuguese voyage to that part of the world. Though it was not identified by the author there seems to be little doubt that the voyage described was that of either Coelho or Jaques. The theory that the existence and whereabouts of an inter-oceanic strait was known before Magellan's voyage, seems to rest largely upon the evidence of these globes. The weakness of the theory lies in the fact that on both globes the passage is shown in latitude 45°S., that is, some 450 geographical miles north of the real strait. Moreover, on both globes another strait between "Oceanus Occidentis" (Atlantic) and "Oceanus Orientalis" is depicted with equal boldness at the northwestern end of the continent in or about latitude 12°N.

On all the old voyages of discovery, time was a vital factor because of the difficulty of provisioning the ships for long periods. For this reason alone, if Magellan had had any convincing evidence even of the approximate whereabouts of the passage he sought, he would surely have steered a more or less direct course, well clear of the land, until he reached the approximate latitudes. Instead of this he chose the far more difficult, dangerous and time-consuming alternative of hugging the coast. This is probably the strongest evidence of his ignorance.

On January 10, 1520, the fleet reached Cape Santa Maria in latitude 35°S. This promontory had been discovered some years before by Juan de Solis, a Portuguese captain of a Spanish ship, who was killed by natives on the shores near by. Before his death, however, he had seen that the coast-line beyond the Cape ran in a direction slightly north of west, which suggested that he might have reached the southern extremity of the Continent. However Magellan may have regarded this possibility, it seems certain that he nursed at least some hope of finding a way through at this point, for he spent three weeks exploring the coasts before he was satisfied that they enclosed nothing but a vast estuary, now known as Rio de la Plata. Even if he himself had not expected a successful outcome to the reconnaissance, the disappointment must have sapped the morale of his crews, following as it did the anxious weeks of navigating the dangerous shoal waters of the bay, often less than three fathoms deep.

Barely 150 miles beyond the southern portal of the estuary the coastline again turned westward, and for more than 300 miles they sailed in that direction with mounting hopes. Again they were dashed; and yet again when, on February 24, they entered the great gulf of San Matias, hoping, always hoping, that here at last was the end of this interminable land whose desolation chilled the heart and which became ever more repellent as they travelled south. It was already two months since they had left Santa Lucia Bay, and there can scarcely have been a man among them who did not long

with all his soul to return to its comfort and plenty. Then, on top
of all these disappointments, all the toil and anxiety of inshore
navigation on an unknown coast, they were called upon to face the
bitter cold of the approaching antarctic winter, cold such as few
of them can have experienced before and which they certainly
cannot have expected in latitudes equivalent to their own home-
lands.

During the whole of March they battled against violent gales and
mountainous seas, soaked by icy spray, in constant danger of ship-
wreck on the rocky coast, always without hot food because of the
impossibility of lighting fires in the galleys. Several times they were
driven back by the headwinds and their groping southward progress
became slower than ever. A landing party sent ashore in search of
fresh water was marooned on a rocky islet where their boat was
smashed by a sudden squall. Their rescue was delayed by the
mounting storm and they survived only by burying themselves under
the carcasses of seals they managed to kill. On another occasion
the fleet sought shelter in a narrow bay only to find no secure anchorage. For six days they were held in this "Bay of Toil", before
a lull in the storm allowed them to escape. At length, on March 31,
in latitude 49°20′S, they found a deep estuary protected by sand-
banks from the ocean rollers; and there—Port San Julian of evil
repute—Magellan decided to spend the winter.

It is difficult nowadays even dimly to appreciate the courage
demanded of these early explorers. The ever imminent destruction
of their clumsy, fragile ships may perhaps be equated with that of
the merchant convoys in the last war, the calculated risks with
those of the astronauts; we may shudder at the months of exposure
to cold and wet, or stand aghast at the hideous privation they had
to endure; but, for the combination of all these factors, wrapped in
the immensity, the terrifying immensity, of the unknown, for this
we have no modern yardstick. Supposing it existed this strait
they sought, supposing against long odds they survived its passage,
what terrors awaited them beyond? Pack-ice more dense than that
of the Greenland coast? Storms more savage, doldrums more life-
less than any in the known world? What new land-mass might bar
their way; why should they expect to be able to sail northward
again to escape from this awful wilderness? Moreover, though the
astronomers amongst them might have good reason to suppose that
by sailing westward they would eventually return to the east, it
had yet to be proved, and the large majority had to take this pre-
posterous belief on trust.

Small wonder that there was clamorous demand from the hard-pressed crews that this crazy enterprise should be abandoned. What is astounding is that Magellan, who could no longer pretend to know the whereabouts of the phantom strait, had won and retained in the face of so much adversity the loyalty of so many of his men that he was able to quell the mutiny which broke out barely two days after they anchored in Port San Julian.

It was instigated by the four senior officers of the fleet, Quesada, Mendoza, Cano and Cartagena (who had been freed from bondage some months before, but not restored to his command). On the morning of April 2, Magellan awoke to find *Victoria, Concepcion* and *San Antonio* in rebel hands. In a situation which must have seemed hopeless both to his enemies and his friends he remained quite unruffled. That very morning, by a subtle stratagem, he succeeded in capturing *Victoria*; and at the same time his flagship and the small *Santiago* were moved athwart the entrance of the harbour so as to prevent the two remaining rebel ships from escaping. For the rest of the day, ready for immediate action, he awaited events. At midnight a powerful ebb tide was running out of the estuary; *San Antonio* dragged her anchors and drifted rapidly towards the flagship. When it was close alongside, Magellan ordered a broadside to be discharged to clear her decks, while he himself led a boarding party. They met with no resistance and Quesada, who had taken command of the vessel, was forced to surrender. With the tables thus decisively turned Cartagena and Cano, who were aboard *Concepcion*, had no option but to follow suit. In little more than 24 hours from its start, the mutiny was over.

Only two casualties had resulted from the whole affair: the loyal first officer of *San Antonio* had been killed at the start, and Mendoza when his ship, *Victoria*, had been taken. At the enquiry held the following day, forty-four officers and men were found guilty of mutiny and sentenced to death; but most of them, after suffering harsh punishment, were spared by Magellan, perhaps more from motives of expediency than of clemency. Quesada was beheaded and his body, together with that of Mendoza, was drawn and quartered and hung on gibbets. Cartagena, a Spanish nobleman of high degree and former second-in-command of the fleet, was condemned to be marooned on that desolate shore. A priest, Sanchez de Reina, who had been a trouble-maker since the voyage began and was one of the ring-leaders of the mutiny, shared his fate.

Though his swift victory over the mutineers had greatly strengthened his hand, Magallan must have been well aware of the delicacy of his situation. Already he had been forced drastically to reduce the consumption of his basic supplies, and the long months of waiting in this bleak spot, coupled with the nagging uncertainty of their future would be a severe strain on his men. Even his most loyal supporters urged him, if not to abandon his quest, at least to retreat to Brazil for the winter. Little time would be lost by such a manoeuvre, it would give the crews a chance to recover their health and spirits and put them in good heart to resume the voyage in the spring. But the Captain-General was inflexible; he judged that, apart from the hazards of such a diversion, any temporary return to the flesh-pots at this juncture, far from raising morale would be more likely to undermine it. The experiences of many later navigators in these waters have shown how right he was.

He seems to have realised what many leaders placed in similar circumstances have failed to appreciate: the vital necessity of keeping his men fully occupied; that active hardship is a great deal easier to bear than passive endurance. For the first few weeks there was no lack of important work to be done: the ships had to be careened and repaired (the exceptionally large tidal movement at Port San Julian and its sandy shores offered excellent facilities for these tasks); huts were erected to accommodate the crews ashore, and supplies of fuel collected from the brushwood which grew on the surrounding land. Luckily the estuary contained plenty of fish, seals and wild-fowl, and large numbers of them were secured not only for immediate consumption but for salting down and storing in the ships' holds. Also the skins of the seals and birds provided material for the manufacture of warm clothing. It is curious that no guanaco was found, for even today these creatures, which closely resemble the llamas of Bolivia, abound in that vicinity.

Towards the end of April, Magellan sent Serrano in *Santiago* to reconnoitre the coast to the south, hoping no doubt that he would find the elusive strait. After sailing for a fortnight against strong headwinds the little ship reached the mouth of a large river sixty miles from Port San Julian, which Serrano named Rio Santa Cruz. There he found excellent anchorage and such large quantities of fish and seals that he spent six days laying in a supply. Some fifteen miles farther south, on May 22, the vessel met with a violent storm which damaged her rudder and drove her ashore. In a few minutes she was smashed to pieces, and though only one of the crew (the Captain's negro slave) perished, nothing was salvaged from the wreck. Twelve days later, far spent with exposure and hunger, the thirty-seven survivors struggled back to Rio Santa Cruz, where they

were able to subsist on fish and seal meat. From there Serrano sent
his two strongest men on in a desperate attempt to reach Port San
Julian. At first they tried to follow the shore where they might
expect to find shell-fish and possibly seal; but soon they were stopped
by marshes and were forced to strike inland where they had no
food and scarcely any water. In their exhausted condition it took
them eleven days to cover the distance which, by the way they
went, must have been about a hundred miles. Prevented by stormy
weather from putting to sea, Magellan sent a rescue party overland,
and eventually all the castaways were brought back.

For many weeks it seemed that the land was uninhabited, but
about mid-winter some people arrived at the estuary. Most of the
men were six feet tall; to the Spaniards and Portuguese of that day
they seemed like giants, and in subsequent accounts their size was
grossly exaggerated. They were shod with moccasins of guanaco
skin which left huge footprints in the sand. For this reason Magellan's
men called them Pata-gon (big feet) and for this reason the land
became known as Patagonia. At first the relations between the
Europeans and the natives were cordial; but Magellan apparently
thought it his duty to take some of the strange creatures back to
Spain, and with this in view he kidnapped two of the young men.
Not surprisingly this put an abrupt end to the cordiality, and it
seems that the memory of the treacherous act was handed down
through many generations of the tribe, as later voyagers were to
find to their cost. Little is known of the fate of the two captives, but
it is believed that one starved himself to death and the other died
several months later.

On August 24, the fleet left Port San Julian and, after a rough
passage, anchored in the mouth of Rio Santa Cruz, where greater
supplies of fish and seals were to be found. Meanwhile the two
mutineers, Cartagena and Reina, had been marooned at Port San
Julian, their slender chance of survival reduced still further by the
hostility of the natives. The captains of all four of the remaining
ships were now Portuguese; *Concepcion* was commanded by Serrano,
Victoria by Magellan's old friend and kinsman Duarte Barbosa, and
San Antonio by Alvaro de Mesquita. They remained at their new
anchorage for nearly two months before the wintery weather showed
signs of moderating. During this time further attempts were made
by some of the officers and pilots to persuade Magellan to abandon
his quest for a westward passage and to sail to the Spice Islands by
an easterly route. However he remained as adamant as before,
saying that if necessary he would follow the coast as far as latitude

75°S before giving up the search. This statement has also been used as further evidence that he did not know of the existence of a passage.

At last, on October 18, after six and a half months in winter quarters, anchors were weighed and the voyage was resumed. For two days, against strong headwinds, the ships struggled yard by yard for southerly progress. Then the wind shifted to the north and they ran before it along the coast. On October 21, in latitude 52°30', they rounded a sharp headland ("Cape of the Eleven Thousand Virgins"), and entered yet another deep gulf. Beyond its entrance the coastline could be clearly seen stretching away to the south, while some thirty miles to the west, the gulf appeared to be enclosed by an unbroken line of low cliffs. Though it seemed to offer little prospect of success, it had to be explored like all the other bays that had raised their hopes. So, while *Trinidad* and *Victoria* anchored under the lee of the Cape, Magellan sent the other two ships forward to reconnoitre.

That night it started to blow hard from the east and by morning the wind was so strong that *Trinidad* and *Victoria* were forced to abandon their anchorage and beat far out to sea to avoid being trapped in the bay. They lost touch with each other and when eventually the storm abated and they reunited in the bay, *Concepcion* and *San Antonio* were nowhere to be seen. It seemed certain that they had been driven on to the farther shore and wrecked. Five days had elapsed since they had started on their reconnaissance. As Magellan's two ships were approaching the western extremity of the bay, which still looked like an unbroken coastline, a column of smoke was seen rising from the land beyond.* This was taken to be a distress signal from the survivors of the disaster. It must have been a bitter moment for Magellan, for he can hardly have hoped after such a catastrophe to rally the shattered morale of his men. Then suddenly, to their utter astonishment, the two missing ships hove in sight from behind a promontory, speeding towards them under full sail, their cannon booming, their yards decked with flags and bunting. It was not long before Serrano and Mesquita were aboard the flagship telling their astonishing tale.

On the evening of October 21, they had anchored under that very headland on the southern shore, close to the western extremity of the bay. By then they were almost certain that it had no outlet in that direction. As we have seen, during that night it started to

* It may well have come from fires lit by Fuegan Indians, a sight with which the explorers were later to become familiar.

blow from the east and by dawn the wind had greatly increased. Fearing to be trapped on a lee shore they weighed anchor and endeavoured to beat to eastward. But they were too late, and before long they found themselves being driven helplessly before a screaming gale. It seemed that nothing could save them from being hurled ashore at the western end of the bay. Miraculously, both ships weathered the headland, and there before them the terrified crews saw a narrow channel running towards the southwest. Still largely out of control and propelled, apparently, as much by the current as by the wind, the ships were swept into and along this remarkable corridor. It became more and more restricted as they went, but after what must have been an alarming run of ten miles, they were shot out into a large, oval-shaped lagoon, twenty miles long and nearly as wide. Beyond this they entered a second channel, wider than the first, which in turn led them into a broad reach which stretched away to the southern horizon.

How long this helter-skelter voyage lasted; at what point the crews regained full control of their ships; where they eventually found anchorage; the answer to none of these questions can be found in the records. It was abundantly clear to the captains that this time they were dealing with no mere river estuary. They had sailed some eighty miles westward from the Atlantic, and the water was as salty as the ocean. Moreover, they observed that the flood tide was at least as strong as the ebb, and this could only mean that the channel they were in had an outlet into another sea. This, surely, was *El Paso* at last, the passage of their dreams; and they had stumbled on it almost by accident! As soon as the wind changed to a favourable direction, they hastened back to report their momentous discovery.

The fleet passed safely through the First and Second Narrows and, on October 28, anchored off an island beyond (probably Elizabeth Island). Then, full of hope that the worst of their troubles were over, they sailed on into the open water which stretched away to the south. Presently, however, their optimism was replaced by renewed anxiety. They had been convinced that they were already through the Strait and expected at any moment to reach the great ocean beyond, the open road to the tropical islands which nine months of bitter hardship had made infinitely desirable. Now, one after another, disturbing features began to erode their confidence. First there was the land to starboard, so drearily reminiscent of the coast they had been following for all those months, stretching on and on to the south. Then there was the wide opening to port with an apparently limitless extent of sea beyond. Was that the right course to follow? Finally there was the dark mass which loomed ahead and gradually resolved itself into a range of mountains. Hitherto the land, though desolate, had been gently contoured; this was something far more sinister. When they drew near they saw that the coast was split by innumerable waterways which penetrated, far beyond their range of vision, into the rugged mountain country. Behind stood icy peaks, one of them a sharp spire so lofty that it seemed to pierce the very sky. How could they hope to find a way through this monstrous labyrinth?

The dejection caused by these fresh discoveries was all the more poignant by contrast with the certainty of success which it replaced. It must have been about this time that Magellan held a conference with his captains and officers to discuss the situation and hear their views. He can hardly have been surprised to find a strong body of opinion in favour of abandoning the search. The most outspoken of those who held this opinion was Estavo Gomez, the Portuguese pilot of *San Antonio* and one of the best and most experienced seamen in the fleet. He argued that even if a way were found without further difficulty, their provisions were already far too depleted for them to undertake a long voyage across an unknown ocean; any serious delay either by storms or calms would almost certainly result in all of them dying of hunger. It would be far better, he said, to go back to Spain and return later with a fleet equipped and able to exploit their discovery. The conference, however, like others that had preceded it, seems to have been a mere formality and it ended in the same manner. Magellan, ignoring all counsel of caution, simply announced that they would go on as he had promised the King, even if they had to eat the leather on the ships' yards. They were prophetic words, for this is precisely what happened.

Again the fleet was divided; *San Antonio* and *Concepcion* were sent to explore the fjords leading to the south and southeast, while *Victoria* and the flagship steered west-northwest into a channel which was seen running in that direction. There were several openings along its southern shore, but as none of them offered a tempting alternative, the two ships held their course for thirty miles and anchored at the mouth of a small river on the northern shore. This was named River of Sardines, because of the great shoals of small fish in the bay. It was by far the pleasantest spot they had encountered since leaving Santa Lucia Bay more than ten months before. By contrast to the stark desolation of the land they had gazed at for so long, the mountainsides, though steep, were covered with forest, green and soft to the eye, which extended right down to the shores. There was fuel in plenty to replenish their stocks and cascades of clear water to fill their casks. Pigafetta's delight was expressed in his journal, "I believe that there is no more beautiful strait in the world". It is possible, however, that this was written several days later for, lovely though the bay may have been, the appearance of the channel ahead was anything but encouraging.

Thus far it had been straight and wide enough to allow reasonable room for manoeuvre; but a few miles beyond the anchorage it divided into two narrow passages, mere slits which, like all the fjords they had seen to the south, disappeared into high, mountainous country beyond. To attempt to penetrate such restricted waters with clumsy sailing ships was at best an extremely hazardous undertaking, particularly amongst high mountains where winds are always erratic. As, in any case, he had to await the arrival of the other two ships and hear the result of their explorations, Magellan decided to make a reconnaissance of the way ahead. For this task he despatched a longboat under the command of Gonzales Espinosa, who had already shown himself to be his most loyal and ardent supporter.

Meanwhile the crews of *Trinidad* and *Victoria* were kept busy catching large quantities of the small fish in the bay and preserving them in salt. Many of the sailors were sardine fishermen by trade, so there was no lack of skilled hands. For Magellan it was a time of supreme anxiety; for he knew that upon the result of Espinosa's reconnaissance and the reports of the captains of the other two ships depended the success or failure of the entire enterprise, the realisation or the ruin of his life's ambition. He did not have to wait long for, according to the chronicles, three days later, Espinosa returned with the wonderful news that he and his crew had sailed right through the channel and had reached the great ocean beyond.

If we accept, as most historians have, the fact that this reconnaissance took only three days, it must surely stand as one of the most remarkable feats in the annals of navigation. It entailed a voyage, to the sea and back, of *two hundred and fifty nautical miles*, the whole of the outward journey through unknown waters. Certainly at that time of the year in latitude 53°S the days would have been long and only a small part of the nights dark enough to prevent movement. The tidal currents in that part of the Strait are exceptionally strong, but their timing was unknown, and even if the longboat party had made full use of the favourable tides they must have been virtually immobilised while the contrary currents were running. Even allowing double the stated time it was a very impressive achievement and can only have been performed in exceptionally favourable weather conditions.

In the various accounts of Magellan's passage through the Strait, apart from the initial storm, surprisingly little reference is made to the weather. In view of what we know of prevailing conditions it seems reasonable to infer from this that it was exceptionally fine throughout most of November 1520. The fact that, despite considerable time spent in reconnaissance and other delays, the entire passage took only thirty-eight days supports this conjecture. Had conditions been anything like normal it is hard to believe that even Magellan would have succeeded in finding and forcing his way through.

We are told that his iron reserve broke down when he heard the news that the longboat had actually reached the western sea, and that he wept with emotion; but his joy must surely have been chilled as he listened to the detailed report of the reconnaissance. No sailor of Espinosa's experience can have underrated the formidable nature of the task ahead. Certainly he was ignorant of the prevailing northwest wind which blows, often for many weeks on end and with great force, for nine tenths of the year; but even without this knowledge the difficulties were alarming enough. For fifty miles the channel was so narrow as to allow no room whatever for the ships to manoeuvre, which meant that no forward progress would be possible except with a fair (more or less easterly) breeze. The precipitous sides plunged steeply into the water so that it would be difficult if not impossible to find anchorage or shelter from sudden squalls; while the forty-foot tides caused wildly erratic currents and eddies. Beyond the fifty-mile reach, though the channel widened considerably, it was beset with islets and reefs. It was a daunting prospect.

There was, however, more immediate cause for concern. Nearly a week had elapsed since the fleet had divided and there was still no sign of the other two ships. Presumably Magellan had ordered them to meet him in the vicinity of the Sardine River well within that period, for he set out with both his ships to look for them. He was anxious no doubt to waste as little time as possible before tackling Espinosa's passage—or an easier one if such could be found. Before long they met *Concepcion*; but Serrano, her captain, had not seen *San Antonio* since the start of his southerly reconnaissance.

On hearing this news Magellan sent *Victoria* back to the Second Narrows in case there had been a misunderstanding about the rendezvous, while he and Serrano made an extensive search of the southeasterly channel which the missing ship was supposed to have been exploring. There is no record of how long this took or exactly where they went, but it is reasonable to assume that, believing the vessel to have been wrecked, they sailed to the extremity of Admiralty Sound before giving up the search. One wonders what they thought of the huge glacier front in Ainsworth Bay, which was probably far more extensive even than it is today, or of the vast ice-fields beyond. Once again it is probable that the weather was fine, for otherwise the search would have taken far longer than is compatible with the overall period. At length, finding no trace of the missing ship, Magellan was forced to conclude either that she had been lost with all hands or that she had deserted.

It was as well, perhaps, that he never learned the truth. Three days after *San Antonio* had left the others, Gomez had staged a successful mutiny. No doubt he took full advantage of the sharp disappointment which must have resulted from the discovery that the southeast channel was yet another cul-de-sac, for he seems to have had little difficulty in persuading the majority of the officers and crew to join the insurrection. Mesquita was made prisoner; the ship was sailed back through the eastern narrows to the Atlantic and reached Spain on May 6, 1521, some six months later. To justify their action the mutineers claimed that the flagship had failed to keep the rendezvous and that they had searched the channels for her in vain. They proceeded to blacken Magellan's name, accusing him not only of great harshness and cruelty but also of gross mismanagement of the whole expedition.

The loss of *San Antonio* had a chilling effect upon morale in the three remaining ships. Far more serious, however, was the fact that she had been carrying a very large proportion of the fleet's supplies which, even before the calamity, had been dangerously low. Magellan was now faced with an appalling dilemma. To set out with barely two months' food across an ocean of unknown size, with no knowledge whatever of the prevailing winds and other navigational hazards, with no means even of calculating longitudes, would be a desperate gamble. To return from the threshold of the greatest geographical discovery ever made would be heartbreaking. Moreover he must have been well aware that if, as he suspected, *San Antonio* had in fact deserted, she would reach Spain long before he could hope to do so, and that he would have little chance of defending himself against the calumnies and misrepresentations of the mutineers. Nothing but spectacular success could save him from his enemies at home.

Once again, on November 20 in the Bay of Sardines, he held a conference of his senior officers. This time he required them to state their views in writing. Unfortunately only one of these statements survived the voyage, that of Andres de San Martin, the astrologer, who was far from sanguine about the wisdom of going forward. Whether or not the majority shared his pessimism, Magellan's reply was characteristic. God, he said, who had brought them to the discovery of the Strait would, in His own good time, lead them to the realisation of their desires. The following day anchors were weighed and the little fleet entered the western narrows.

It is tantalising to have no record of their passage through this critical section of the Strait. Having slammed the door behind them, what were their feelings during those anxious days as they groped their way through the baffling currents of that landlocked channel towards the unknown hemisphere beyond? Wonder? Elation?—Or were these emotions eclipsed by fear? In all history it would be hard to find any just comparison, any apt analogy, with their situation.

We may assume that the weather was fine and that they could see far up the many fjords piercing the great forests and ice-fields in the interior of Isla Santa Ines, which to this day is still largely unexplored. It was among these fjords, apparently, that they saw the many fires which led Magellan to give the name "Tierra del Fuego" to this southern land. It has been said that he believed it to be an island or archipelago and not part of the legendary continent, *Terra Incognito Australis*. If this were so, it must have been pure conjecture and not, as we are told, because he heard the roar of breakers from a hidden sea beyond the mountains. Of the Alakaluf Indians who made those fires he saw no other sign.

On November 28, he sailed past Cape Desire into a sea so tranquil that he called it *Mare Pacifico*: it is strange indeed that it should thus have derived its name from one of the most tempestuous regions on earth. From there he steered north and west across the ocean "more vast than the imagination of man can conceive"; on through torments of famine and thirst to death and immortality.

On September 8, 1522, almost three years after the start of the voyage, *Victoria*, the only remaining ship of Magellan's fleet, dropped anchor in Seville harbour. She was commanded by Juan Sebastian del Cano, one of the ringleaders of the San Julian mutiny. There were only eighteen survivors on board.

3 Drake and Sarmiento

IT IS A MEASURE of the immense value of the 16th century spice
trade that, despite the appalling losses in men and ships suffered by
the expedition, the cargo brought back in the holds of the little
Victoria yielded a substantial overall profit for its backers. In other
respects, however, the results of the venture were far from beneficial
to Spain, and there were innumerable occasions during the next
hundred years when her citizens had reason to curse the discovery
of Magellan's Strait.

A conference held at Badajoz to determine the rightful ownership
of the Moluccas failed to reach agreement. Spain's claim was based
on the geographical position of the Islands, east of the 120th
Meridian E., while that of Portugal was backed by prior possession.
To strengthen his position, Charles V despatched, in 1525, another
fleet of five ships and 450 men by way of the newly discovered
Southwest Passage. It was led by Garcia de Loaysa with Sebastian
del Cano as his second-in-command. Whatever may be said about
Cano's mutinous conduct at Port San Julian, one has to admire the
spirit which sent him on this second voyage barely three years after
surviving the ghastly ordeals of the first. He had been richly rewarded
both with money and honours and might well have been content
to rest on his laurels. Several more of his sixteen fellow survivors
joined him.

The expedition was an unqualified disaster. After a gruelling
struggle lasting three months, four of the ships passed through the
Strait. On the long haul across the Pacific most of the company died
of scurvy, including Loaysa and Cano, and only two ships and one
hundred men reached the Moluccas. In their enfeebled condition
they were no match for the Portuguese, now well established in the
Islands, and none of the ships returned to Spain.

Although shortly after this fiasco, King Charles yielded to Portugal
all Spanish claim to the Moluccas, during the next fourteen years
there were five more attempts to use the Southwest Passage as a
means of access to the Pacific and the Far East and, by 1540, a

total of twenty-one ships had been employed in the endeavour. Twelve had been wrecked in or near the Strait, and of those which actually reached the Pacific only one, Magellan's *Victoria*, had returned to Europe. Of the men who had taken part in the ventures, more than two thousand had perished, and only some twenty per cent had regained their native shores. They were discouraging statistics even for the spice-crazed merchants and hardy seamen of the 16th century, and it is not surprising that for a long while Magellan's great discovery was shunned. Moreover, as the years went by, the tales of the survivors lost touch with reality, and so gave rise to legends which did much to enhance its horrific reputation.

Meanwhile the conquest of Mexico by Cortes and of Peru by Pizarro had provided Spain, with access to riches even more dazzling than those of the Spice Islands—and much more accessible. The gold and silver brought down from the Andes were transported to Panama in coastal vessels built on the shores of the Pacific. They were virtually unarmed, partly from the difficulty of supplying them with cannon, mainly because there seemed no reason to do so. The precious metal was carried, largely by slave labour, through the fever-ridden swamp and forest of the Isthmus—"thirty miles of misery"—to fortified towns on the Caribbean coast, where it was loaded into heavily armed galleons for the final stage of its journey. The Pacific empire of Spain, the source of this vast wealth, continued to expand and prosper, secure behind the growing tradition that the southern Strait was closed.

It was not until the end of the 15th century, after the long agony of the Wars of the Roses, that England turned her attention to seafaring, a way of life which was to play so great a part in her destiny. Soon, English merchants and seamen began to covet a share in the wealth of the Orient; but though they did not acknowledge the exclusive right bestowed by the Pope upon Spain and Portugal, they were not yet nearly strong enough to challenge it. Other ways must therefore be found; and so were born the ideas of the "Northeast Passage" and the "Northwest Passage" to the Pacific. The search for these elusive waterways, starting with the voyages of Chancellor to the east and of Frobisher to the west, continued intermittently for more than three hundred years. In material terms it yielded a very lean harvest.

A more profitable alternative was piracy, which in Elizabethan England acquired a mantle of respectability from her increasing hostility to Spain. But though Spanish treasure ships were considered fair game, the practice of sailing the galleons only in large, heavily armed convoys made attack difficult and hazardous; while such escapades as Drake's raid on the Panama Gold Road, though immensely rewarding if successful, relied too much on the element of surprise to be often repeated. Thus the scope for large-scale privateering in the Atlantic was rather limited.

It was on the occasion of his famous attack at Nombre de Dios that Francis Drake, like Balboa, first saw the Pacific Ocean from the saddle of the Isthmus, and it was this that inspired his ambition to reach it by way of Magellan's Strait and to attack the treasure train at its unprotected source. The idea of making the second circumnavigation of the Globe was an afterthought dictated by circumstance. At 32, Drake was already well-known as a daring and skilful seaman and with this asset he was able not only to get the private backing he needed for his venture but to win the tacit approval of the Queen herself. Naturally the object of the expedition had to be kept secret even from the sailors, and it was put about that Alexandria was the destination of the fleet. This was composed of four small ships—*Pelican*, 100 tons; *Elizabeth*, 80 tons; *Marigold*, 30 tons; *Swan*, 50 tons; and a pinnace. The total complement of 164 men included a number of "gentlemen adventurers" who, though for the most part ignorant of the sea, had probably invested money in the enterprise. Among them was Thomas Doughty, a man with friends in high places, who may well have helped Drake to make influential contacts.

The fleet set out in December 1577. On the way along the coast of North Africa various Spanish fishing and trading vessels were seized, perhaps more for the sport afforded than for the value of the cargoes. At the end of January, near the Cape de Verde Islands, a more important capture was made: a Portuguese ship "laden with singular wines and many other good commodities which stood us in that stead, that she was the life of our voyage". Still more valuable was the acquisition of her pilot, Nuño da Silva, whose extensive knowledge of the Atlantic coast of South America was a great help. The rest of the crew were put ashore on one of the islands while the ship (renamed *Mary*) and the pilot were added to the strength of the fleet. Some fifteen months later da Silva was released in Guatemala and shortly afterwards produced a detailed account of his experiences which was both objective and notably free from rancour.

On April 14 the fleet reached the Plata estuary where Drake called a fortnight's halt for recuperation. Several times in the stormy weather which followed *Swan* and *Mary* became detached from the others and as a result of these delays, it was June 20, mid-winter, before the ships reached Port San Julian. It is improbable that Drake had originally intended to spend the winter in this ominous place. Being more or less compelled to do so, however, it is conceivable that he deliberately chose it for the scene of the crisis which had long been brewing. His career offers many other examples of his strong sense of dramatic occasion.

So many conflicting accounts have been written of the trial and execution of Thomas Doughty that it is almost impossible to form a clear impression of the story. Perhaps the simple statement of Lopez Vaz comes nearer to the heart of the matter than all the complicated speculation which has been lavished upon the affair. In an account of the voyage written less than ten years later he dismisses it in a single sentence: "Francis Drake sailed unto Port San Julian, where he wintered: and there he put to death a gentleman of his company, *because he would have returned home*". A world of meaning is contained in those six words.

Even under the paltry stresses of modern expeditions, we know how a man can behave when faced with unexpectedly harsh conditions; how sometimes, when the spirit dissolves, a violent reaction of self-justification sets in and with it obsessive dislike of the author of his misery. We can hardly suppose that men in the 16th century were immune from this weakness, particularly when confronted with a combination of hardship, danger, privation and tedium almost unimaginable today. Doughty was a courtier, a politician, a man of private means, not a professional sailor. He was certainly brave, but whatever his motive for joining the expedition, adventure, financial gain or political advancement, he may well have underestimated the rigours of such a voyage. That he acquitted himself well enough during the first few weeks is clear from the fact that, for a while, Drake gave him command of the Portuguese prize, *Mary*. But lighthearted piracy on the Barbary Coast was a very different matter from months of storm and tempest in the South Atlantic, an ordeal itself a mere foretaste of the horrors to follow.

Doubtless there were many others who "would have returned home" if they had been given the chance; and therein lay the danger. For, unfortunately, Doughty was a man of considerable influence, with the wit to seduce and the money to suborn, and known to have had a large stake in the expedition. Moreover, according to the social order of the time, he was far superior to the little upstart adventurer who now controlled his destiny, and who expected gentlemen to "hale and draw" with common seamen. It is not

difficult to understand the temptation to use his power to spread
and foster dissension as the only means of escape from his intolerable
situation.

For Drake, at the most critical stage of his great enterprise, it
was a matter of supreme importance that he should have the
complete confidence and loyalty of his men. Though his situation
was not quite comparable with Magellan's in that the way to the
Pacific had been found, it was precarious enough. The grim record
of disaster connected with the Strait, the fact that no one had
attempted the passage for nearly forty years and that in the meantime its reputation had assumed the quality of an evil legend, these
were matters not easily dismissed from the minds of men about to
embark upon months of inactivity on a desolate, wintery shore, men
moreover who had been unaware of their destination until after they
had left their homeland. On this fertile ground Doughty had sown
the seeds of discord and defeatism, and such conduct by a man in
his position could only be construed as mutiny.

Drake conducted the melancholy affair with his usual panache.
The most bizarre episode occurred shortly before the execution
when he and the condemned man dined together and toasted each
other in an atmosphere of relaxed cordiality. Certainly Doughty
seems to have behaved with remarkable dignity, and his last request
was that those who had supported his indiscretions should be
forgiven. That his gallantry won him a great deal of sympathy is
shown by the accounts of several eye-witnesses highly critical of
Drake's action. Meanwhile the Admiral, having made his point,
must have felt himself in a very strong position for, at the end of an in-
spiring speech to the assembled company, he actually offered to make
Marigold available to anyone who still wished to return home. As
no doubt he had confidently expected, there were no takers.

Because of the frequent delays he had suffered from the dispersal
of the fleet in foul weather, Drake decided to reduce it to more
manageable proportions by abandoning two of the ships, *Mary* and
Swan. With the three remaining vessels he sailed from Port San
Julian on August 17 and reached the entrance of the Strait some
five days later. There, with due ceremony he renamed his flagship,
Golden Hind, from the family crest of one of his principal backers,
Sir Christopher Hatton.

Drake had the good fortune to meet this southern land in one of
its gentle moods and the passage of the dreaded Strait was achieved
with such ease that it must have been something of an anti-climax.
A light northeasterly breeze wafted the ships through the First and

Second Narrow and they anchored off Elizabeth Island (so named by Drake) where, in balmy spring weather, the crews spent a day catching several thousand penguins "whose flesh is not much unlike fat goose here in England" to augment their food supplies. Reaching the open water beyond Cape Froward, Drake was puzzled: "we had such a shutting up to the northwards, and such large and open Frates toward the South, that it was doubtful, which way we should pass". He seems to have been already convinced that the rugged land to the south was an archipelago. He decided, however, despite its unpromising appearance, to follow the northwesterly channel, where "the mountains arise with such tops and spires into the aire, and of so rare a height, as they may well be accounted among the wonders of the world".

It was in that section of the Strait that Drake and his men made the first recorded contact with the canoe Indians (presumably Alakaluf) of Tierra del Fuego. Francis Fletcher, the Chaplain, found them "a comely and harmless people . . . gentle and familiar to strangers". Though this scarcely accords with the opinions of later observers, his account ("The World Encompassed") of the habits of these strange people and their nomadic way of life is remarkably accurate and perceptive. He made a complete inventory of the contents of one of the wigwams (belonging, he thought, to the "Chiefest Lord"), which he valued at 25 pence. He was particularly struck by the excellence of their canoes which were made from pieces of bark sewn together with strips of sealskin. They were fashioned with such skilful craftsmanship that he considered them more suitable "for the pleasure of some great and noble personage" than "for the use of so rude and barbarous a people".

According to da Silva's log, Drake's passage of the Strait took fourteen days; Fletcher's account made it two days longer. In either case it was an astonishing performance, particularly at that time of the year, several weeks before the vernal equinox, when the daylight hours were still short. Except for some reference to strong headwinds which sometimes forced the ships back, we know little about the weather which was encountered and it may be assumed that, as with Magellan, it was unusually fine. Also Drake's ships were far smaller and more manageable than those of his predecessors. But even with these advantages the feat could not have been accomplished without the most daring and highly disciplined seamanship.

On September 6, the ships entered the Pacific. Drake had intended to land at Cape Deseado, there to place a monument in honour of the Queen and to commemorate his voyage. But with a strong breeze blowing and seeing no suitable anchorage he decided to forego this gesture and continued on his *northwesterly* course for the next two days. Possibly his intention in so doing was to gain plenty of searoom before turning northward; for he must have been well aware of the prevalence of westerly gales in those latitudes. But when the ships were some two hundred miles beyond the exit of the Strait, they were struck by a storm, "the like whereof no traveller hath felt, neither hath there been such a tempest, so violent and of such continuance since Noah's flood; for it lasted full 52 days".

At first the gale, accompanied by alternating rain and snow, blew from the northeast and for three weeks the ships, bare of sail, were driven southwestward before the mighty blast. On the night of September 15–16, in a momentary clearing, the moon was seen in partial eclipse. A fortnight later *Marigold* lost touch with the others and was never seen again. Probably she sank in the mountainous sea; possibly, dismasted, she drifted to the southeast eventually to be cast upon some remote Antarctic island. For, shortly after her disappearance, the wind shifted to the west which enabled the other two ships to start beating back to the northeast. They had reached latitude 57°S.

On October 7, almost a month since the storm began, land was sighted and that evening the battered vessels found precarious refuge from the still raging storm in a bay formed by a group of rocky islets a little to the north of the Strait. But no sooner had they dropped anchor than they were smitten by a squall so violent that *Golden Hind*'s cable parted and she was hurled southward once more. The next morning, John Winter, *Elizabeth*'s captain, finding the flagship vanished from sight, sailed into the Strait and anchored in an open bay near its exit. During the two days they stayed there his crew kept large fires burning ashore in the hope that the smoke would be seen by their missing companions. Then he moved to a more sheltered harbour further in the Strait. He called it the Port of Health, "for the most part our men being very sick with long watching, wet, cold, and evil diet, did here wonderfully recover their health. . . . Here we had very great mussels, (some being twenty inches long) very pleasant meat". After waiting there for three weeks and believing that Drake and his men had perished, he set sail for home. Later he came in for some criticism for this decision, for Drake had issued specific orders that any ship which became detached should proceed to a rendezvous point in latitude 30°S on the Pacific coast. Incidentally, by his eastward passage of the

Strait, Winter refuted the belief, current at the time, that it was impassable in that direction.

Meanwhile Drake had been driven southeastward along the coast of Tierra del Fuego. In a clumsy, topheavy ship of 100 tons, with her crew already exhausted by more than four weeks of shattering storm, striving desperately to keep clear of the myriad reefs and islets of that villainous shore, yet searching amongst them for a refuge from the intolerable wind, groping blind through the equinoctial nights, still more than ten hours long, it was a struggle for survival as critical as any in his reckless career. It is difficult to tell from Fletcher's horrific account of the hurricane how long this particular ordeal lasted. We know that at one point, presumably during a brief lull, the ship approached close enough to the coast for a boat with eight men to be sent ashore for fresh water; but before they could return a revival of the gale forced Drake to stand out to sea leaving them stranded. By a miracle—a series of miracles —we know what became of the unfortunate castaways.

Later, in latitude 55°S Drake found brief respite in a wide channel among the islands (possibly Desolate Bay) where, going ashore, his exhausted men experienced their first moments of relaxation for many weeks. There, besides fresh water, they found "diverse good and wholesome herbs", including one "not unlike that which we commonly call Pennyleaf, which purging with great facility, afforded great help and refreshing to our weak and sickly bodies". After only two days, however, the storm returned with all its former ferocity and dragged them out once more into "the most mad seas" where "the winds were such as if the bowels of the earth had set all at liberty". By then there can scarcely have been a man aboard who had not abandoned hope of survival; indeed they were so numbed with cold and crushed by fatigue that it is doubtful if any much cared.

At last, on October 28, the storm subsided. But for a few brief lulls, it had raged for more than seven weeks. It was then, after perhaps the finest feat of seamanship of his whole career, after one of the outstanding examples of dogged endurance on record, that Drake made his momentous discovery. No wonder that he discerned the hand of God in his recent ordeal! For, when the weather cleared, he found himself to the eastward, but still within sight, of the southernmost islands of the Fuegan archipelago. Beyond was a vast expanse of sea where the Atlantic and the Pacific "meet in a most large and free scope".

Returning westward in fair weather, Drake dropped anchor under the lee of the most southerly island of all, and went ashore to indulge in one of those dramatic gestures so dear to his heart. Compass in hand, he sought out the southern extremity of the island. There he lay on his belly and wriggled forward until his head and shoulders were projecting over the sea. Then he returned to his ship with the delighted boast that he had been further south on land than any other man. A petty gasconade? Perhaps; but it showed a strong sense of situation which must surely be shared by most explorers. Despite his accurate reckoning of its position (56°S) and a mass of other evidence, some historians have been at pains to argue that the place where Drake performed his ceremony was not Cape Horn (so named in 1616 by Jacob le Maire after his ship, *Horne*, which in turn he had called after his native village). Even if they are right it does not alter the fact of Drake's discovery, the immense significance of which, both geographical and political, he himself was at once aware.

After two days among the southern islands, which he named "Elizabethides", Drake returned along the coast of Tierra del Fuego, now warm and inviting in the spring sunshine. He stopped in one of the channels to collect a great quanity of birds before sailing on to launch his devastating attack upon the western Spanish Main.

It must have been on this very day that Captain Winter abandoned all hope of seeing his chief again and started on his return voyage. At the same time the eight castaways, having recovered from the first crushing realisation of their plight, were doubtless looking about for means of survival. They had been marooned at the height of the storm on a sub-antarctic shore whose very existence was hitherto unknown; they possessed nothing but an open boat, probably about fifteen feet long, their knives and the saturated clothes they wore—no food, no tentage, no bedding, no firearms. Day after day, night after night the tempest continued to rage— perhaps a week, maybe two—and there was nothing for them to do but to cower behind whatever shelter they could find and cling to their ebbing lives.

At last the ghastly storm subsided, the screaming wind was hushed, the sky cleared and the blessed sun came to quicken their numbed bodies and dry their clothes; some sweetness returned to life and with it hope—forlorn perhaps, but even a glimmer seems bright after the darkness of despair. Though the world they were in was wild, rugged and lonely, it was not without its friendly aspects. In the sheltered coves and glens there were green woods, deep beds of moss, brightly flowering shrubs and clear streams, balm to the senses of men who had been so long at sea. Moreover there was food enough in the form of shellfish and crabs as well as edible roots and herbs. They also seem to have had, or later found, the means of making fire.

Having acquired some mastery of their environment they set out on their formidable journey. How they reached the Strait of Magellan is not known. Perhaps they followed the coast back to Cape Deseado, though this would have been a perilous voyage in a rowing boat, involving a long stretch of open ocean against the prevailing wind. Perhaps, wandering through the intricate passages among the islands in search of food, they stumbled upon one of the channels through the Fuegan archipelago: Abra Channel, for example, which remained unknown until the late 19th century, or Barbara Channel, surveyed by Skyring in 1828. Whichever way they went, it is strange that they appear to have met with only one party of Fuegan Indians, who fled at their approach.

Once in the Strait they were in familiar surroundings. With their tiny boat they could find shelter in the smallest coves and, by taking advantage of favourable weather and tides, make steady progress. At "Penguin Island" (presumably Drake's Elizabeth Island) they spent some time salting and drying enough of the birds to last them until they reached Port San Julian where, with improvised hook and line, they caught abundant fish "like Breames and Mackerils". Farther north, on the off-shore islands of the Patagonian coast, "we killed a good store of seals to our sustenance, the young ones we found best and ate them roast". Eventually, after rowing more than two thousand miles, they reached the River Plate. Here, when they might reasonably have expected an easing of their trials, they met disaster.

Landing on the northern coast of the great estuary, they went into the forest along the shore to look for food. There they met a party of some sixty natives who immediately attacked them with bows and arrows. They were all "grievously" wounded, and four were captured. The remaining four managed to get back to the boat and escape to an uninhabited island some ten miles from the shore, where two died of their wounds. Shortly afterwards the two survivors, Peter Carder and William Pitcher, suffered further calamity when their boat, their precious boat which had served them throughout their incredible voyage, was smashed to pieces in a storm.

During the next two months they endured the worst of all their hardships—extreme thirst. For food they had small white crabs and eels, which they dug from the sand, and a fruit resembling a small orange; but there was no water whatever on the island, and no rain fell. Though they imbibed a certain amount of liquid from the fruit it was totally inadequate, and their thirst became so intolerable that they drank their urine, having first cooled it overnight—"which being drunk often, and often avoyded, became in a while exceeding red".

Eventually they found a plank ten feet long, washed up on the shore, which, together with some smaller pieces of wood, enabled them to construct a raft. On this they embarked, taking with them a small supply of crabs, eels and fruit. After three days and two nights on this clumsy contraption they reached the mainland close to a stream of sweet water. Tormented by thirst, Pitcher fell on his face and drank and drank and drank. Realising the danger of overindulgence by men in their condition, Carder tried to persuade him to stop, but the wretched man refused to listen and half an hour later he died.

Having buried his friend with "unspeakable grief", Peter Carder set off "along the shore towards Brazil". The following day he fell in with another tribe of people known as Tuppan Basse who, though they turned out to be cannibals, treated him with warm hospitality and with whom he lived for many months. He learnt their language and taught his hosts several useful skills including the construction of shields to withstand the arrows of their enemies. These were a great success and were largely responsible for an overwhelming victory against a neighbouring tribe in which Carder seems to have played an active part. Many of the captives taken in the battle were roasted and eaten. The same fate befell "certain Portugals and Negroes" who were unlucky enough to fall into the hands of the tribe.

Some time after this he persuaded the grateful King of the Tuppan Basse to allow him to depart. Not only was his request granted but he was provided with four men to escort him and keep him provided with food for the first ten weeks of his journey north. In this way he succeeded in reaching the Port of Bahia, latitude 17°S, in Brazil. There his prospects seemed as bleak as ever; for, on the grounds of his illegal entry into Portuguese territory, the Governor decided that he should be imprisoned and sent to Portugal to serve as a galley slave for the rest of his life. Happily his cause was espoused by a wealthy land- and ship-owner, Antonio de Pava, who, "could speak good English and was a lover of our Nation".

This excellent man persuaded the Governor to allow Carder to work for him pending the decision of higher authority in Lisbon.

For some two years he was employed, first as overseer on Pavo's estates, then in a small vessel plying between various ports in Brazil. Then he learnt that the Governor's decision had been ratified and that he was to be sent to Portugal forthwith. However, with the help of his patron, who had warned him of this impending doom, he contrived to escape and to remain in hiding until he had the opportunity to board a small vessel bound for Europe. Near the Azores she was captured by two English men-of-war, and on November 25, 1586, nine years after sailing with Drake from Plymouth, Peter Carder reached Chichester Harbour. Thence he was taken by Lord Howard, the Lord High Admiral, to Whitehall where he was commanded to relate his strange adventures to Queen Elizabeth in person.

Drake had reason to be well satisfied as he sailed along the coast of California, hoping to crown his great enterprise with the discovery of the Northwest Passage. His ship was deeply laden with plunder of immense value, and his avowed intention "to annoy" the Spaniard had been achieved in spectacular fashion. His raids had been conducted with such skill that, though they had spread terror and consternation throughout Spain's Pacific empire, little blood had been shed. Far greater misery and loss of life were to result from the aftermath.

Don Francisco de Toledo, Viceroy of Peru, was faced with a difficult situation. The loss of so much treasure, the humiliating defeat of Spanish might by a single ship and a few dozen men, the complete impotence of his armed forces to retaliate, these were galling enough; but they were of small account beside the appalling implications of the affair. If Drake could find his way through the "impassable" Strait, other English or French privateers could follow; indeed more ships of his own fleet might already be lurking, ready to pounce upon any of the settlements along the coast. For these were almost devoid of the only protection against such attacks —artillery; and a mere handful of hostile ships armed with cannon would have them all at their mercy, thus amputating the main source of Spanish wealth.

The Viceroy decided that the best way of dealing with this emergency would be to establish a settlement at some suitable point within the Strait of Magellan, sufficiently fortified to block the passage of any hostile fleet. With this object in view he sent two ships under the command of Pedro Sarmiento, with instructions to make a detailed exploration of the Strait and of any possible alternative entrances and passages, and to select a suitable site for the proposed settlement. This must, of course, be in a narrow section which could not be by-passed. On completing this task Sarmiento was to send one of the ships back to Peru with copies of his reports and charts while he himself was to sail on to Spain to place his findings before the King who, in the meantime, would have been informed of the Viceroy's proposal.

Pedro Sarmiento was a man of remarkably varied accomplishment. After serving five years as a soldier in Europe he went to Mexico and thence, in 1557, to Peru where he seems to have held some office at the viceregal court. For ten years he devoted most of his energies to compiling a history of the Incas. His interest in the occult brought him into serious conflict with the Inquisition, from which he was rescued only by the intercession of influential friends. He was also a gifted mathematician and had at some period made a deep study of the theory of navigation, which enabled him, in 1567–9, to play a leading part in a voyage of discovery to the Solomon Islands. His distinguished career, however, was marred by the atrocious cruelty he displayed in the ruthless persecution and murder of the last of the Incas. It was said that, because of this, a curse fell upon him; and no doubt the legend gained currency from the extraordinary record of disaster which marked much of his subsequent life. "The luck of Sarmiento" became a term synonymous with great misfortune.

Immediately after Drake's raid on Callao (the port of Lima) in February 1579, Sarmiento was employed in an unsuccessful chase after "the English pirate", and it was not until October 11 that he set out on his important and extremely arduous mission. His deputy was Juan de Villalobos who commanded the second of his two ships. By November 17 they had reached latitude 50°S where Sarmiento decided to begin the first part of his task, a detailed examination of the coast in search of alternative passages leading to Magellan's Strait. Entering the Gulf of Trinidad he succeeded, with considerable difficulty, in finding safe anchorage for his two ships.

From there, during the next two months, accompanied by two pilots and a dozen sailors, he made three long boat journeys through the bewildering labyrinth of channels and islands to the south. Each voyage, some two weeks long, was attended by all the misery, the cold, the gales, the lashing rain, so often encountered on that part of the coast, each was accompanied by almost daily threats of disaster and by spells of semi-starvation. Physically it was a fine performance for a middle-aged man (he was 47), whose life hitherto had not inured him to this kind of hardship. But what made it unique was the quality of the survey he achieved which, in the accuracy and minute detail of his observations and in the clarity of his descriptive records, was nearly two centuries ahead of its time. Moreover, he evidently became so fascinated by the exploration of the region that, despite the vile conditions and the formidable tasks ahead, he extended his investigations far beyond the needs of his prime objective. In this he was defeated by the sheer size of his task; though, from his farthest point—*Ancóns in Salida* (Bay without Outlet)—at the northern tip of the Muños Gamero Peninsula, he looked down Smyth Channel which was first traversed 250 years later and is now the main route for shipping.

It is hardly surprising that, when he returned from the last of his boat journeys, he found much discontent in the two ships. Two months of idleness in a desolate cove had been hard to bear, particularly as there seemed little to be gained by the detailed exploration of such a wild and useless region. Villalobos voiced the opinion, shared by many others, that as so much time had been lost, the expedition should be abandoned; and when, on January 21, the ships sailed from the harbour and ran into a northwesterly gale he seized the chance to desert. That night he returned to the shelter of the islands and, when the storm subsided, headed back to Peru.

For two days Sarmiento was driven southward, blinded by mist and spray. On the morning of the 23rd, the weather cleared and he sighted a headland behind which he managed to find refuge in a protected cove which he named Bay of Mercy. "That night we were like deaf men in the fine weather, but it did not last long for the next morning there arose such a gale of wind that the sea would assuredly have swallowed us up if we had been outside." The renewed storm continued to rage for the next eight days and with such force that despite the sheltered position the crew had great difficulty in holding their anchorage. Only when the gale had finally abated and Sarmiento was able to see something of his surroundings did he realise that the headland was none other than Cape Deseado. But for that chance clearing on the morning of the 23rd, he would certainly have been carried far to the south and probably destroyed by the storm which followed. Evidently the curse of the Incas had not yet begun to work.

The crew, however, had been badly shaken by their recent experiences and they were in a rebellious mood. They refused to believe that they were actually within the entrance of the Strait, and even the pilots were sceptical. Meanwhile Sarmiento had to postpone his advance; for though he already suspected that his consort had defected he could not be sure. It had previously been arranged between the two captains that if their ships were separated they would meet at the mouth of the Strait, and that the first to arrive would wait at least two weeks for the other. However, after making a reconnaissance by boat, he moved his ship eastward to a more comfortable anchorage. It may have been the very place where Winter had waited for Drake; for he learnt from some Fuegans whom he met there of a recent visit by bearded strangers resembling his own men, though it was impossible to obtain any detailed information about them.

Before leaving Peru the possibility of his meeting with hostile ships had been considered, for it was known that Drake had originally been accompanied by other vessels which might still be lurking somewhere on the coast. In the orders he had received from the Viceroy, Sarmiento had been told to use his own judgement in this eventuality, unless the intruder should prove to be Drake himself; in which case the "pirate" was to be attacked whatever the risk. In fact Sarmiento can have had little fear of this, for he was aware that Drake was hoping to return home by way of the Northwest Passage. Indeed there is some evidence to suggest that Sarmiento himself believed in the existence of that northern route to the Pacific. If this were the case it is surprising that he maintained his belief in the importance of his own mission. Had he known of Drake's discovery of the way around Cape Horn, he would certainly have realised its utter futility, and thus averted untold misery.

Pedro Sarmiento's account of his eastward passage of the Strait of Magellan contains the first clear description of the famous channel. Once again he displayed his genius for accurate, co-ordinated observation and close attention to detail. Here, as with his survey of the archipelago south of Trinidad Gulf, he set a standard of coastal charting hitherto unknown. It was this that won him a place among the great navigators of history and the homage of British naval explorers of the 19th century.

Viceroy Toledo's proposal to fortify the Strait had been opposed by some members of the Royal Council. Rumours, however, began to circulate that the English were planning to seize the passage; and when in August 1580 Sarmiento reached Spain and presented an optimistic report on the feasibility of planting a settlement on the shores of its eastern section, King Philip decided to proceed with the project. Thus it was that on September 25, 1581, a massive expedition of twenty-three ships and more than 3,500 people sailed from San Lucar under the command of Diego Flores de Valdes. Having reached the Strait and landed the garrison and settlers (which included forty-three women and eighty-seven children), the fleet was to be divided into three detachments; one to proceed westward to strengthen the garrisons on the Pacific coast, the second to return to Brazil under Flores, while the third was to remain at the disposal of Pedro Sarmiento who had been appointed Governor of the Strait.

The ensuing voyage was marked by a series of disasters rarely equalled in the annals of the sea. Barely a week after its departure the fleet met with a storm in which five of the ships were sunk, two were damaged beyond repair and eight hundred lives lost. After returning to Cadiz for repairs, the remaining sixteen vessels made a second start; but it was not until March 24, after further heavy loss, that the expedition reached Rio. Flores, who had as little liking for his task as he had aptitude for naval command, decided to wait there for seven months to avoid reaching the far South in winter. The following November passing the mouth of the River Plate in calm weather the largest ship sprang a leak and sank so rapidly that 330 men and twenty women were drowned. The rest were taken back to a harbour on the coast of Brazil, where yet another vessel was wrecked. So the dismal toll of death and destruction continued to mount until, out of the twenty-three ships that had left Spain, only five remained.

At length, on February 7, 1583, they reached Magellan's Strait and anchored in the First Narrow. That night, however, they were driven out to sea by a westerly gale, and after struggling for more than six weeks to regain the entrance, sailed all the way back to Rio. There they found four ships which had been sent from Spain with stores and equipment for the projected settlement. Flores, however, had had enough and, nominating one of his officers, Diago de Rivera, to take his place, he returned home. Though the terrible calamities suffered by his fleet were mainly due to his total incompetence, this does not seem to have incurred any loss of prestige; for, five years later, he was given high command in Philip's attempted invasion of England, a responsibility which he discharged with equal lack of distinction.

In December the five ships again sailed southward from Rio. This time they were favoured by fine weather; on February 1, 1584, they reached the Strait and, the very same day they passed through the First Narrow on the flood tide. It seemed that, with the departure of Flores, the fortunes of the expedition had turned at last. But they had scarcely dropped anchor before a combination of a strong westerly wind and the powerful current of the ebb tide carried them back through the Narrow. To avoid being driven out to sea, Rivera took his ships into a small bay, two miles west of Cape Virgins, where Sarmiento disembarked with three hundred of his people to found the first settlement. Before the stores could be landed, however, a westerly gale dragged all five ships from their anchorage and they disappeared beyond the Cape. When, a week later, they returned to discharge their cargo, one of them was driven ashore and wrecked. No lives were lost and, though much of the food was spoilt by sea water, the rest of her cargo was salvaged. But before this was done, Rivera, doubtless demoralized by these events, slipped away during the night with three of the remaining ships and a quantity of stores intended for the settlement, leaving his colleague to make the best of an unhappy situation.

Five years had now elapsed since Drake's raid upon Callao had first involved Sarmiento in this sorry affair; three years had passed since he had received his royal commission. After all this time, after all the hardship and frustration he had endured, here he was, Governor of the Strait, with one small frigate and a pathetic mob of four hundred men, women and children, lamentably ill-equipped and furnished with perhaps six months' provisions. They were certainly in no condition to bar the Strait against hostile ships, and unless help arrived they could have no concern but for their own survival. Moreover, with the southern winter only a few weeks away, even their immediate prospect was far from bright. Nevertheless, Sarmiento set them to work to build what he called the "city" of Nombre de Jesus, but which can hardly have consisted of more than a collection of stone and mud shelters; one of them, duly consecrated, served as the church.

While passing through the Strait four years before, Sarmiento had found an excellent site for his settlement at Cape Santa Ana, near the southern end of Brunswick Peninsula, where the land was sheltered, fertile and well wooded. At the end of February, he despatched the frigate, *Maria*, to this place with half the available stores and equipment, and on March 4 he set off overland with a hundred men for the same destination. The men were supplied with four pounds of biscuit each, which many of them consumed in two days, after which they had to subsist on shellfish and such berries as they could find. Beyond the First Narrow they met a tribe of natives who were friendly at first but then launched a vicious attack, killing one Spaniard and wounding ten before they were repulsed. After a week the men's shoes were worn out and most of them had to march with bare feet. Beyond the Second Narrow they were forced by a series of inlets to make long detours inland, and for several days they found nothing to eat but berries. On March 20, spent with fatigue and hunger, they reached the harbour behind Cape Santa Ana where they found the ship. In sixteen days' march over a rough terrain they had covered, according to Sarmiento's estimate, over 300 miles. Besides the man killed, six more had been left to die on the way.

For the survivors the move had been well worth while, for their new environment was far pleasanter than the bleak, treeless, windswept land surrounding Nombre de Jesus. There was also much more food available. Sarmiento speaks of the country abounding in large deer (guanaco, perhaps) "which stood until we approached quite close . . . and many birds, which is a sign that there is plenty of fruit in the woods . . . and many flocks of green parakeets. . . . There are also many shellfish . . . the soldiers and sailors cooked them in a stew with wild cinnamon . . . and plenty of fish". In view of this abundance the men (about 130 including the crew of *Maria*) were each issued with twelve ounces of flour a day while the other imported foodstuffs were conserved. All were busily employed building the new "city" of San Felipe; here the church, the municipal buildings and the dwelling houses (one to four men) were constructed with local timber (*notho fagus: antarctica* and *betuloides*) and thatched with reeds. Also the ground was dug and planted with grain and vegetable seeds which, alas, did not prosper.

While all this was going on some of the soldiers planned to seize the frigate and sail it back to Brazil forcing the pilot to go with them. They were handicapped by the fact that, since the vessel could only carry a very small proportion of the settlers, their scheme was not likely to commend itself to the majority who might otherwise have been only too happy to join in the mutiny. As a result Sarmiento was informed of the plot, the ringleader was executed and his head stuck on a pike.

Towards the end of April winter was ushered in by a snowstorm which continued without interruption for fifteen days. Though the scene was transformed, Sarmiento was enchanted to find that many of the trees retained their green foliage. He now decided to return to Nombre de Jesus to arrange for some of the settlers there to be transported to San Felipe, and then to examine the possibility

of building forts on the shores of the First Narrow. Together with
thirty of his men he set sail at dawn on May 25 and, with a fair
breeze and taking advantage of the tides with which he was now
well acquainted, reached the anchorage at Nombre de Jesus after
dark on the same day. Soon after the vessel had anchored two men
came aboard with a message from Captain Viedma, the officer in
charge of the settlement. His news was far from cheerful. Apart from
intermittent skirmishes with native tribes the settlers had suffered
a great deal of hardship; they were thoroughly depressed, some had
mutinied and Viedma had executed the ringleader. This was
Sarmiento's last contact with the people who had been placed under
his care; for, before the messengers could disembark, a violent gale
sprang up, the anchor cable parted and the little frigate was driven
out to sea.

For three weeks Sarmiento and his crew struggled against the
storm trying to regain the Strait. At length it was lack of food—
"with only half a barrel of flour and roots . . . some became blind
with cold and hunger"—which forced them to abandon the attempt
and sail northward to Brazil. They reached Santos on June 27.
Sarmiento then decided to bend all his efforts to get help for the
unfortunate people marooned in the Strait. He sailed on to Rio
where, with the assistance of the Governor, he arranged for a small
ship laden with flour to be sent. Some months later he learned that
she returned with her cargo, having failed to reach the Strait.
Meanwhile he sailed north in search of further provisions, clothing
and other necessities, taking a cargo of Brazil dye-wood for their
purchase; for it seems that not even a Governor in dire distress was
entitled to requisition his colleagues' supplies.

While so engaged the frigate, *Maria*, was wrecked off the coast
near Bahia; several of the crew were drowned, but Sarmiento was
saved by floating ashore on a plank. However, the Governor of
Bahia provided him with another ship of 160 tons and having
procured from other benefactors the supplies he needed, he sailed
southward once more, calling at Rio on the way. But now the tide
of his misfortune was flowing at full strength. In latitude 33°S, he
was struck by yet another storm of such severity that he was forced
to jettison most of his precious cargo and limp back to Rio with a
badly damaged ship.

Nearly two years had now elapsed since his involuntary departure
from Nombre de Jesus; yet another southern winter was about to
begin; and when at length, with further help from the Governor of
Rio, his ship had been refitted and loaded with more supplies, the

crew refused to embark upon another attempt to reach the Strait. Sarmiento was already deeply overdrawn upon the generosity of his colleagues in Brazil; moreover news had arrived from Spain that the King was thoroughly dissatisfied with the conduct of the Strait project, which would make it even harder for him to raise credit. In view of all these circumstances he decided that his only course was to return to Spain to explain the desperate plight of the settlers and to implore the King to send a well-equipped relief expedition without delay. With this object, he sailed from Brazil on June 22, 1586.

On August 11, near the Azores, he was attacked by three English men-of-war under Sir Richard Grenville, who was on his way home from Virginia. Resistance was useless and the wretched man was taken to England a prisoner. Here, however, he had a brief respite from his troubles. A fortnight after his arrival at Plymouth he was sent to Hampton Court and taken under the care of Sir Walter Raleigh who seems to have found him excellent company and treated him more as an honoured guest than a captive. The Queen herself expressed a desire to meet the Governor of Magellan's Strait and he "conversed with her in Latin for more than two hours and a half, in which language she is proficient". Moreover she granted him permission to leave the country and return to Spain and, on top of all this, presented him with a substantial sum of money—"a thousand escudos". Perhaps this bounty was intended as a last minute gesture of conciliation to King Philip with whom she was already virtually at war.

So, on October 31, 1586, Sarmiento crossed the Channel to Calais and set out on the last stage of his long and eventful journey. But it was another three years before he saw his native land; for on his way across France he was seized by the Huguenots who, pending the negotiation of a suitable ransom, kept him incarcerated until the end of 1589. During much of that time he was kept in conditions of such hideous squalor that he must often have wished himself back among his people at Nombre de Jesus. Despite his own torment he contrived to spare much thought to their suffering which he voiced in a series of pitiful letters to his King urging him to send relief. Philip, however, had too many important matters on his hands, including his catastrophic attempt to invade England, to trouble about a few hundred starving subjects. No action was ever taken.

At dawn on May 26, 1584, some two hundred and fifty people had looked out from their huts at Nombre de Jesus across the gale-swept

bay to find that the little ship *Maria,* their only means of contact
with the outside world, had vanished in the storm. As the dark winter
months dragged by it became increasingly hard to support life on
that desolate shore, and in August Viedma decided to evacuate the
settlement and move everyone to San Felipe. But when, after a
heartbreaking trek, they arrived there, it was only to find that food
was just as scarce. Indeed the concentration of so many people in
one place made the situation still more critical, and two hundred men
were sent back to Nombre de Jesus. None of them was heard of
again.

For those left at San Felipe, the summer of 1584/85 brought some
relief from their hardship; but no vessel came to their rescue and
when winter returned they sank into deep despair. Many died,
doubtless as much from sheer dejection as from actual want. The
living were too listless to remove the dead with the result that their
dwellings became uninhabitable. By the following summer fifty men
and five women were still alive, and Viedma set them to building
two boats. These were completed by the autumn (early in 1586) and
they all embarked, apparently with the intention of sailing westward through the Strait. The weather was fine, but apart from
Viedma himself there was no sailor among them, and before they
had gone twenty miles one of the boats was wrecked. The project
was abandoned and they spent the ensuing winter in small groups
spread out along the coast, hoping in this way to secure a more
plentiful supply of shellfish.

Early in the summer of 1586/87, at the time when Sarmiento was
being entertained at Hampton Court, a pitiful band of eighteen
survivors, fifteen men and three women, reassembled at San Felipe;
Viedma was among them. In December, they set off along the coast
towards Nombre de Jesus. It is difficult to guess the purpose of the
journey, since they can hardly have expected to find in that direction
any alleviation of their suffering; and if they needed a reminder of
this it was there in the daily sight of skeletons strewn along the shore.

By the evening of January 6, they had reached a point beyond
the First Narrow. There they saw three ships sailing towards them
from the open sea. At nightfall they anchored off the southern shore
of the bay, and the Spaniards, half-crazed with the anticipation
of relief, lit fire signals and received answering lights from the ships.
The next morning, to their joy, they saw a boat lowered from one
of the vessels and rowed in their direction; but presently it turned
westward toward the Narrow. Viedma ordered a young officer,
Tomé Hernandez, and two soldiers who were still sufficiently

active, to follow the boat and try to make contact with the occupants. They ran along the shore and succeeded in reaching the headland at the northern entrance of the passage just as the boat was approaching close in shore. It was then that they learnt with dismay that the ships were English.

The squadron, which had sailed from Plymouth six months before, was commanded by Thomas Cavendish, whose purpose was to emulate Drake's raid upon the Pacific coast. Before leaving England he had heard something of the disasters which had befallen Sarmiento's attempt to found a settlement in the Strait, and he may well have gathered further information during his southward voyage. When, therefore, on the morning of January 7, he went with the boat to reconnoitre the Narrow, he was not altogether surprised by the appearance of three ragged, emaciated men, frantically hailing him from the headland. Approaching the shore, he told them that if they cared to embark they could have a passage to Peru. They replied that they did not wish to do so, "because they feared that they would be thrown into the sea"; to which Cavendish retorted that they need have no fear since the English were better Christians than the Spaniards. This curious dialogue was conducted through an interpreter who happened to be in the boat. On second thoughts the men decided to entrust themselves to the dreaded English as the lesser of two evils, and the boat came in to pick them up.

When Hernandez had explained the situation, Cavendish told him to send the two soldiers to fetch their fifteen fellow survivors so that they, too, might be taken to Peru. He then returned to his ships with Hernandez and, finding the breeze and tide favourable for his advance through the Strait, made sail and departed forthwith, apparently without the slightest compunction, leaving the wretched Spaniards, fourteen men and three women, to add crushing disappointment to their burden of misery.

It is hard to find excuse for his behaviour. Writing early in the 19th century, Captain (later Admiral) Burney attempts to do so by pointing out that the passage of the Strait was so precarious and examples of failure so numerous that Cavendish would have been heavily blamed if he had missed his chance for the sake of an act of rescue. "From these considerations it may be argued that the English, in not staying to relieve the Spanish colonists, did not act in a manner repugnant to the general practice of the most civilized nations". He adds, however, "Considering the shortness of the required detention, the extraordinary hardships they had endured and their extreme distress, it must excite some wonder that the claims of humanity did not prevail". Some wonder indeed!

The following day the squadron reached "Penguin Island" where, once again, huge numbers of birds were killed and added to the ships' stores. Five days were spent at San Felipe taking in wood and water. There, in the corpse-strewn "city", was revealed the full horror of the tragedy. Cavendish called the place "Port Famine"; and the name, in English and Spanish, has been retained ever since. Some months later, on the coast near Valparaiso, Hernandez contrived to escape and join his compatriots. With them he ambushed a shore party from the ships; twelve English sailors were killed, nine more were captured and later hanged.

On January 1, 1590, a ship named *Delight*, commanded by Andrew Merrick, entered the Strait from the Atlantic. Near Port Famine she picked up the sole survivor of Viedma's little band. The last of his companions had died more than two years before. Thirty miles beyond Cape Froward the vessel met with a severe northwesterly gale, in which she lost all her boats and anchors. She was forced back and, after a terrible return voyage, reached Cherbourg on August 30 with only six of her company left alive. Neither Merrick nor the Spaniard was among them.

4 Stokes in *Beagle*

MANY of the great episodes of history have been set in motion by trivial and seemingly unrelated incidents; but there can be few more striking examples of this than in the story of *Beagle*. The famous voyages of this little ship covered a period of ten years; they resulted, only because of a strange series of accidents, in the emergence of one of the great figures of the 19th century and a revolution in scientific thought.

By the end of the Napoleonic wars British sea power was at its zenith. During the decades which followed, the high standards of initiative, morale and seamanship forged by the Royal Navy during the long, hazardous campaigns were fruitfully employed in voyages of geographical exploration and scientific investigation. The most spectacular of these were the renewed attempts to discover the Northwest Passage to the Pacific, a project which had been largely abandoned since Elizabethan times. The expeditions of Ross and Parry, the terrible land journey by Franklin and Back, the vanishing of the first Polar steamships, *Erebus* and *Terror*, into the silent Arctic wastes, and the twelve years' search for them which followed; together they make up one of the most remarkable chapters in the annals of human endeavour. It is a story of appalling hardship and danger, of striving and frustration, of miraculous escape and frequent tragedy, in which the deeds of heroism performed by naval officers and seamen alike match any in the preceding wars.

While this Arctic drama was being enacted, other ships of the Royal Navy, notably H.M.S. *Challenger*, were engaged in long voyages to remote parts of the Globe, mapping uncharted coasts for the benefit of international shipping and reaping a rich harvest of scientific data. If their exploits were less spectacular, their tasks, in some cases at least, were scarcely less exacting.

On May 22, 1826, H.M.S. *Adventure* and *Beagle* under the command of Captain Philip Parker King, sailed from Plymouth Sound bound for South America. They were "well provided with every necessity, and every comfort, which the liberality and kindness of the Admiralty, Navy Board, and officers of the Dock-yards, could cause to be furnished."* *Adventure* is described as a "roomy ship of 330 tons burthen, without guns, lightly though strongly rigged and very strongly built"; *Beagle* as "a well built little vessel of 235 tons, rigged as a barque and carrying six guns".

Captain King was a man of thirty-five who had won distinction and fellowship of the Royal Society by his surveys of the Australian coasts. His instructions were to ascertain the longitudes of Cape Santa Maria and Montevideo, and then to make an accurate survey of the coasts, islands and straits of South America between the estuary of the Rio de la Plata and Chilöe Island (latitude 42°S. on the Pacific side of the Continent), including those of Tierra del Fuego. The direct distance from the Plata estuary to Cape Horn and thence to Chilöe is some 2,200 geographical miles; the length of the coast-line to be surveyed is *many times* that distance; certainly a formidable task for two tiny, square-rigged vessels operating in one of the most tempestuous regions of the world.

The ships sailed from Montevideo on their southward journey on November 14, 1826. The survey of the Atlantic coast of the mainland, which is relatively flat and unbroken, presented no great problem, and King had decided to begin with some of the more difficult parts of his mission, because "the climate of the high latitudes being so severe and tempestuous, it appeared important to encounter its rigours while the ships were in good condition— while the crews were healthy—and while the charms of a new and difficult enterprise had full force." So, except for two stops on the coast of Patagonia to make various observations, the ships proceeded "with all expedition" to the Strait of Magellan.

More than two centuries had elapsed since the notorious channel had lost its strategic importance. For thirty years, Drake's discovery that the Atlantic and the Pacific were joined by a vast expanse of open ocean had remained a secret so closely guarded that not even the English captains who sought to emulate his exploit on the Spanish Main made use of the intelligence. Thus it was not until after 1616, when the Dutch merchant, Jacob Le Maire, found his way eastward round the Fuegan archipelago, that Magellan's Strait, which had taken such an appalling toll of lives and ships, was abandoned in favour of the less hazardous alternative. Since then, Tierra del Fuego, a region of evil legend shunned by all prudent seamen, had acquired a still more sinister reputation when it became the haunt

* Quotations in this and the next two chapters are from *Narative of the Surveying Voyages of H.M. Ships Adventure and Beagle* (3 vols., London, 1839).

of pirates. This began in the late 17th century when a company of eighty French privateers, finding competition in the Caribbean too keen for their liking, moved their headquarters to the Fuegan channels where they remained for seven years, making profitable sorties against ships and settlements on both sides of the Continent and then retreating with their booty to their mysterious hideout. During this time they must have gained an intimate knowledge of the archipelago which, not unnaturally, they never divulged; nor is there any record of which harbours they used, how they contrived to survive, what contacts they made with the natives or of how many pirate bands followed their example.

When, on December 20, 1826, *Adventure* and *Beagle* rounded Cape Virgins, they entered a region famous in the annals of the sea and yet very largely unknown. No wonder "the officers and crew of both ships were elated with the prospect before them." Sailing slowly through the eastern section of the Strait, past many historic landmarks, they reached Port Famine, the site of Sarmiento's ill-fated "city of San Felipe", near the southern end of Brunswick Peninsula. This place, with its excellent harbour, was chosen by King as the main base for his expedition.

On January 15, 1827, *Beagle*, commanded by Captain Pringle Stokes, was sent to survey the western entrance of the Strait, with orders to return on April 1. Leaving *Adventure* in Port Famine, King set out in a small decked boat, *Hope*, into the labyrinth of unknown channels and islands to the south. Passing through Gabriel Channel, a strange, gorge-like passage, half a mile wide, he saw the devastating effect of the whirlwinds, known as "williwaws" or "hurricane squalls", common in the mountainous areas of Tierra del Fuego. Without any warning they strike vertically downwards with great violence, uprooting trees and destroying anything movable; "ships at anchor are sometimes suddenly thrown over on their beam ends."

At the eastern end of the Channel the scenery was magnificent, dominated by towering peaks with, here and there, a glimpse southward to the "icy domain" beyond. "There are upward of a hundred and fifty waterfalls, dashing into the channel from a height of fifteen hundred, or two thousand feet. The course of many is concealed, at first, by intervening trees, and, when half-way down the descent, they burst upon the view, leaping, as it were, out of the wood. Some unite as they fall, and together are precipitated into the sea in a cloud of foam; so varied, indeed, are the forms of these cascades, and so great their contrast with the dark foliage of the trees, which thickly cover the sides of the mountain, that it is impossible adequately to describe the scene. I have met with nothing exceeding the grandeur of this part of the Strait."

Rounding Cape Rowlett, *Hope* entered a wide channel (afterwards "Admiralty Sound") and found excellent anchorage in Brookes Bay. Nearly all the geographical features were named as they were discovered, either after members of the expedition or distinguished sailors, or from incidents which occurred at the time or because their shapes suggested familiar objects. Most of these names have been retained on modern maps.

Both off Cape Rowlett and in Brookes Bay they met with parties of Fuegan Indians and it would be hard to guess whether the British seamen or these strange people were the more intrigued by the encounter. "The Natives", writes Captain King, "conducted themselves very quietly, and, except for one of the women, who wished to keep a tin pot in which some water had been given her, made no attempt to pilfer." He showed commendable tolerance when one of the party "spit in my face; but as it was not apparently done angrily, and he was reproved by his companions, his un-courteous conduct was forgiven." For their part, the Fuegans seem to have been equally forbearing of the strange behaviour of the Captain: "Their astonishment was much excited by hearing a watch tick; but I believe I had very nearly, though unintentionally, given great offence, by cutting off a lock of hair, from the head of one of the men. Assuming a grave look he very carefully wrapped the hair up, and handed it to a woman in the cave, who, as carefully stowed it away in a basket, in which she kept her beads and paint: the man then turned round, requesting me, very seriously, to put away the scissors, and my compliance restored him to good humour."

"The features of these people bore a great resemblance to those of the Patagonian Indians, but in person they were considerably shorter and smaller. The elderly people of both sexes had hideous figures; the children, however, and young men, were well formed. . . . They were clothed, with mantles of guanaco, or other skins, but not so neatly as those of the Patagonians. Their bodies were smeared with a mixture of earth, charcoal, or red-ochre, and seal oil; which, combined with the filth of their persons, produced a most offensive smell. Some were partially painted with a white argillaceous earth; others were blackened with charcoal; one of the men was daubed all over with a white pigment. Their hair was bound with a fillet of plaited twine, made perhaps with strips of bark, and a few of them had it turned up; but to none did it appear to be an object of attention, except one of the young women, who repeatedly

combed and arranged hers with the well toothed jaw of a porpoise.
. . . Their dexterity with the sling is extraordinary; and, I should
think when used as a weapon of offence, it must be very formidable.
. . . I have seen them strike a cap, placed upon the stump of a
tree, fifty or sixty yards off, with a stone from a sling. In using a bow
and arrow, also, with which they kill birds, they are very dextrous.
The spear is principally for striking porpoises and seals, but also
used in war; and from the nature of the barb, must be an efficient
weapon. For close quarters they use clubs, stones held in the hand,
and short wooden daggers, pointed with very sharp-edged quartz,
pitch-stone, or flint."

Happily, on this occasion, the belligerent use of these weapons
was not demonstrated, for, despite the spitting and hair-cutting
incidents, King and his crew soon established cordial relations with
the Fuegans. A brisk trade was conducted in which skins, arrows
and bone necklaces were eagerly proffered by the natives in exchange for beads, buttons and medals which had been specially
struck for this purpose before the expedition had left England. "The
furs which covered their backs they parted with for a few beads,
and went quite naked the whole evening." As neither side knew a
word of the other's language all communication was conducted in
mime, but they seem to have achieved a remarkable measure of
understanding. When the British were preparing to leave Brookes
Bay, the Fuegans did their best to persuade them to stay. The chief
"was very importunate, and at last offered us his wife, as a bribe,
who used all her fancied allurement to second his proposal."

Hope proceeded eastward along the southern shore of Admiralty
Sound and found a secure harbour in Ainsworth Bay. "The bottom
of the port is formed by an immense glacier, from which, during
the night, large masses broke off and fell into the sea with a loud
crash, thus explaining the nocturnal noises we had often heard at
Port Famine" (*85 miles* distant in a direct line!) "and which at the
time were thought to arise from the eruption of volcanoes."

The appearance of low country to the southeast led King to
hope that he would find a passage to the Atlantic in that direction;
but on reaching the head of the Sound he found that there was no
such opening. *Hope* then returned by the way she had come and,
after a further excursion southward through Magdalen Channel,
reached Port Famine by the middle of March.

Soon after his return King received tragic news. Ainsworth,
Adventure's Master, had taken a gig and cutter across the Strait
to survey a part of the coast. On the way back the gig capsized in a

squall, and before the cutter could come to her aid, Ainsworth and two seamen were drowned. The Master died in the act of rescuing another of his shipmates. When the first few days of April passed without sign of *Beagle*, the Captain became anxious; and he was preparing to send *Hope* to search for his consort when, on the 6th, a whale-boat arrived bringing news that all was well.

After a difficult passage round Cape Froward, the southernmost port of the American Continent, *Beagle* had made a fairly rapid passage through the Straits until she was fifty miles from their western exit, where she met with a series of storms. Towards the end of January she succeeded in groping her way to a fairly secure anchorage in Tamar Bay. From there three futile attempts were made to gain further progress; each was beaten back by westerly gales and by heavy squalls of rain and hail. Returning from the first of these in gathering darkness, "while running about eight knots, a violent shock, a lift forward, heel over and downward plunge electrified every one; but before they could look round, she was scudding along, as before, having fairly leaped over the rock." From this encounter they were lucky to escape with only "a great part of the gripe and false keel knocked away."

The second attempt ended when, "about seven in the evening we were assailed by a squall, which burst upon the ship with fury far surpassing all that preceded it; had not sail been shortened in time, not a stick would have been left standing, or she must have capsized. As it was, the squall hove her so much over on her broad-side, that the boat that was hanging at the starboard quarter was washed away. I then stood over to the north shore to look for anchorage under the lee of a cape, about three leagues to the north-west of Cape Tamar. On closing it, the weather became so thick that at times we could scarcely see two ships' lengths ahead. These circumstances were not in favour of exploring unknown bays, and to think of passing such a night as was in prospect, under sail in the Straits, would have been a desperate risk; I was therefore obliged to yield the hard-gained advantage of the day's beat, and run for anchorage whence we had started in the morning." Even so, entering the Bay in the dark, *Beagle* again nearly came to grief when she struck violently on a rocky ledge.

Conscious of the grave risks involved in forcing his ship forward in these conditions without knowing where to find anchorage on either shore, Captain Stokes left *Beagle* in Tamar Bay under the charge of Lieut. Skyring, and set out in the cutter with Flinn, the Master, taking a week's provisions, to make a close examination of the south coast. Beset by a constant heavy gale from W.N.W., thick mist and incessant, drenching rain, it was "a very arduous and dangerous cruise." "Our discomfort," says Stokes, "in an open boat was very great, since we were constantly wet to the skin. In trying to double the various headlands, we were repeatedly obliged (after hours of ineffectual struggle against sea and wind) to desist from useless labour to take refuge in the nearest cove which lay to leeward." Nevertheless they discovered several well-sheltered anchorages along the coast and succeeded in reaching the western exit of the Straits. This daring reconnaissance enabled them to pilot their ship through further storms to Sarmiento's Mercy Bay under Cape Pillar (formerly Cape Deseado), which she reached on February 15. The passage of 155 miles from Port Famine had taken them thirty-one days.

Stokes' main task was to fix the positions of Cape Pillar and Cape Victory, the western portals of the Strait and to chart a group of dangerous islets, known as the Evangelists, which guard the entrance. Luckily, six days later the weather moderated enough to enable him to complete the work, which won this handsome praise from Captain King. "I never reflect upon this piece of service without an inward tribute of admiration to the daring, skill and seamanship of Captain Stokes, Lieutenant Skyring and Mr. Flinn."

At the end of February, *Beagle*, her mission fulfilled, started on her return voyage with plenty of time in hand for further charting of the Straits and to reach Port Famine by the appointed date. But on March 3, near Playa Parda, she met a whale-boat with the mate and five seamen belonging to a British schooner, *Prince of Saxe Coburg*. This unfortunate vessel, with a crew of twenty-two, had been on a sealing voyage in the South Atlantic when she was beset by ice in stormy weather and was forced to seek refuge on the Fuegan coast. She was lying at anchor in Fury Bay, in one of the outer islands of the archipelago, when she was driven ashore by violent "williwaws" and wrecked. The Master and all his crew of twenty-one survived this disaster and, having retrieved three of the ship's boats and most of their provisions, established themselves on shore in improvised tents. During the following weeks, one of the company died, another accidentally exploded a keg of gunpowder and was badly burned, and three more, "being mutinous, were punished by being sent, each to a different island, with only a week's provisions."

With the permission of the Master, seven of the survivors set off in the largest of the whale-boats, to attempt to reach Rio Negro, 40°S on the Atlantic coast of South America, believed to be the nearest point of civilised habitation. Considering that it involved a voyage in an open boat through several hundred miles of uncharted Fuegan channels, constantly at the mercy of storms, followed by a thousand miles along the wild coast of Patagonia, the attempt had little chance of success. Before leaving Fury Bay they drew up "articles of agreement'" for the conduct of the enterprise, a breach of which was to be punished by the offender being left on the coast wherever they happened to be. In fact all seven of the party survived the ordeal and reached their destination. Soon afterwards they volunteered for service with a Buenos Aires squadron then engaged in a war with Brazil.

Meanwhile the other castaways began to build a small vessel in which they hoped to escape; at the same time the Master sent his two remaining boats to scour the neighbouring channels on the off-chance of finding help. Fifteen days later they returned unsuccessful; but after two more abortive attempts, one of the boats was lucky enough to meet *Beagle* on her return voyage from Cape Pillar.

Captain Stokes ran down wind to Port Gallant where he left his ship and set off southward through Barbara Channel with two ten-oared boats, taking *Saxe Coburg*'s mate as guide. Luckily the weather was fine and, despite a delay caused by the mate having forgotten the way, the boats took only two days to cover the eighty miles to Fury Bay, where there was a dramatic meeting with the seven remaining castaways. They had been recently visited by a party of Fuegans and for some reason they were convinced that the natives would soon return in force bent on plunder. So they had buried their possessions and fortified their camp; and when Stokes' two boats appeared they seized their arms and prepared to repel attack. Soon however "excess of joy succeeded their sudden alarm".

After *Beagle*'s return from her adventurous voyage, both ships continued the survey of the eastern section of the Strait and then sailed back to Rio de Janeiro to refit and replenish their stores. Captain King was anxious to obtain a small auxiliary ship to facilitate the survey of the inner sounds and channels of the Fuegan and Patagonian archipelagos, for which neither *Adventure* nor *Beagle* were adapted. Though he had the support of Admiral Otway, C.-in C. of the South American Station, the matter had to be referred to the Lord High Admiral in London. This resulted in a delay of several months, but eventually a suitable schooner was bought in Montevideo and renamed *Adelaide*. Thus it was late December before the expedition sailed southward to resume its work. On her way to the

Strait, *Beagle* surveyed the coast between Port Desire and Cape Virgins, and one of her officers, Lieutenant Sholl, died.

Port Famine was again adopted as the expedition's main base. In March, 1828, having ordered Captain Stokes to proceed with the survey of the Pacific coast of Patagonia, King set out in *Adelaide* to explore a passage, known as "San Sebastian Channel" which, for more than two hundred years, had been supposed to penetrate through the main island of Tierra del Fuego to the Atlantic. It turned out, however, to be nothing but a huge gulf surrounded by low, swampy country, utterly desolate and affording no shelter from the relentless westerly gales. King called it "Useless Bay", a name which it still bears. For the remaining weeks of autumn *Adelaide* was employed in the difficult task of charting the deeply indented eastern coast of Isla Santa Ines, one of the biggest islands of the Fuegan archipelago, whose interior is still largely unexplored. At the end of May the work was brought to an abrupt halt by the loss of a whale-boat, vital for the task of exploring the narrow channels. It happened when *Adelaide* was anchored off Cayetano Island with the boat moored alongside. During a dark night some Fuegans swam from the shore through the icy water, cut the painter and towed their prize away so silently that nothing was heard by the watch on deck. An extensive search of the neighbourhood yielded no sign of the missing boat.

With the advance of winter, life at Port Famine became increasingly hard and monotonous. Heavy snow fell, wet and slushy, and the coast, dreary at the best of times, became even more desolate. Most of *Adventure*'s crew were encamped on the shore; prolonged gales flooded the low ground where their tents stood and spoiled the pond water on which they relied. It was not particularly cold, temperatures ranging between 19°F and 48°F, but the constant damp seeped into their bones. Morale was already low by the middle of June (almost mid-winter) when scurvy appeared and spread rapidly. This was a wholly unexpected calamity and quite unaccountable, for though fresh food in the form of fish and game was now difficult to procure, the men were well provided with antiscorbutic agents such as cranberries and wild cherry. It is even more strange when we consider that at this period the crew of *Beagle* were facing far more severe hardships and privation without suffering from this particular affliction. Perhaps Captain King was right in believing that monotony was a major factor contributing to the sickness among his men. With this in mind he caused a rumour to be spread that the ships would leave Port Famine as soon as *Beagle* returned. "To give a semblance of reality to this report, the top-masts were ordered to be fiddled, and the ship otherwise prepared for sea, which had a manifest effect upon the scorbutics* of which several were in a bad stage of that horrid disease." But as the weeks dragged by with no sign of the consort, the men's despondency became even more marked; two of them died and the sick list continued to grow. By July 25 the situation had become so bad that the Captain issued definite order to "prepare ship for sea". No sooner had the words escaped the boatswain's lips, than "all was life, energy and delight . . . everyone looked forward with pleasure to the change, except myself. I had hoped to pass the twelve months at Port Famine, with the intention of completing a meteorological journal, for which this place afforded peculiar advantages."

On July 27 *Beagle* arrived, and four days later there occurred the tragedy which was to forge the first link in that strange chain of events leading to her immortal fame.

The orders given to Captain Stokes in March 1828 were to survey the Pacific coast of Patagonia from the western exit of the Strait of Magellan, latitude 52°40′S, to the northern point of the Gulf of Penas, latitude 47°S, and to return not later than July 24. It was a formidable assignment, particularly in view of the fact that, by the time *Beagle* sailed from Port Famine, on March 18, the brief southern summer was nearly over. For the first twelve days the passage of the western Strait was a replica of the ship's cruise of a year before: days spent in constant struggle against westerly gales, heavy rain and thick mist which obscured both shores for long spells; nights spent in uneasy anchorages. But at length the weather improved and on the last day of the month she sailed past Cape Pillar on a southerly breeze.

Stokes decided to take advantage of this favourable wind to reach the northern part of the coast assigned to him as soon as possible, leaving the survey of the southern section until the return voyage when he could expect to be served by the prevailing north-westerlies. His luck held for three days and *Beagle* had reached latitude 50°S, when, with the return of bad weather, he found an excellent harbour in Port Henry, at the entrance to the Gulf of Trinidad. During their stay of three days the ship's company were busy surveying the surrounding coasts and collecting supplies of wood, water and fresh food which consisted mostly of mussels, limpets, sea-urchins and young seals; the meat of these creatures

* Sufferers from scurvy.

was considered excellent fare, "not exceeded even by the finest lamb's fry".

They put to sea again on the morning of April 5, and were immediately struck by a violent storm and mountainous seas which continued without respite until the 9th, when a lull enabled them to make a few miles northward progress and to see something of the coast of Campana Island. The need to keep as close as possible to these dangerous leeward shores, studded as they were by innumerable uncharted reefs and islets, so as to observe their features, demanded constant watchfulness and hard work from the crew and imposed a heavy burden of responsibility upon the Captain. The strain, coupled with the physical discomfort, was already beginning to tell and many of the crew were sick with pulmonary and rheumatic complaints. On April 14, after a further series of storms which repeatedly drove her back they managed to bring the ship to an anchorage in a bay at the northern end of Campana Island, where she was held prisoner by appalling weather for the next nine days.

On the 24th, when at last they were able to emerge, they stood straight across the Gulf of Peñas and, during three days of comparatively favourable conditions, explored the coasts around Cape Tres Montes, its northern headland. On the 27th, just before the onset of the next storm, they were lucky enough to discover an excellent harbour in an extensive bay behind the Cape, which they named Port Otway. Here once more they were confined, this time for nearly a fortnight by continuous tempest and incessant heavy rain. But for once they had a really secure, sheltered anchorage, and although the Captain fretted at the delay, the crew enjoyed a sorely-needed rest. Moreover, when the weather moderated they were able to make boat and land journeys around the bay which enabled the surveyors to fix a number of prominent points for use in their subsequent work. The western shores of the bay were so protected that the trees of the forest grew to exceptional size. One day Stokes and Skyring crossed the narrow isthmus connecting the Cape with the mainland. The contrast between the two sides was astonishing: "The inlet where we left our boat resembled a calm and sequestered mountain lake, without a ripple on its waters; the shore upon which we now stood was that of a horrid rock-bound coast, lashed by the awful surf of a boundless ocean."

On May 19, they sailed out of their haven to begin the charting of the Gulf, which has since become notorious for its savage weather. Half their allotted time had already been spent, and all but a tiny fraction of the hundreds of miles of coastline assigned to them had still to be surveyed. With mid-winter barely a month away the days were short and the nights long and very dark. With the constant risk of blundering into a submerged reef or being driven aground by a sudden squall, never knowing where to look for safe anchorage the strain of navigating close inshore was intense. Often they were forced by nightfall to seek refuge in dangerous, windswept coves, often they had to sail through narrow, rock-strewn passages to examine some major inlet beyond. Of one such place Stokes remarks, "nothing would have induced me to enter it, but the duty of examining the coast, and the danger of remaining under sail close to an unexplored shore". And to cap it all the weather, the gale-force winds, the drenching rain, the fog, the cold—not the dry cold of sub-zero temperatures, but a damp, clinging cold which is far, far harder to endure.

Parts of the lowlands of the northeast coast of the Gulf were found to be covered by immense sheets of ice. The explorers were much puzzled by this because they were in the latitude (47°S) equivalent in the northern hemisphere to that of Central France. They were in fact the ends of some of the great glaciers draining from the North Patagonian ice-cap, the existence of which was then unknown. The first time they saw this phenomenon they mistook the ice for a huge bank of sea mist.

On May 26 one of the crew died from 'inflammation of the bowels" (probably appendicitis). Two days later they reached an inlet which they called "Channel's Mouth"; it was the entrance of a fjord stretching 100 miles inland, now known as Canal Baker. There they found good anchorage under the lee of a wooded island. This was fortunate, for they were held there for two weeks by what Stokes describes as "the worst weather I ever encountered", weather in which "the soul of man dies in him". During the whole of that time the ship was battered by squalls of hurricane force, and the rain and hail were indistinguishable from the drenching spray. Despite the protection afforded by the island, the vessel was in constant danger of dragging her three anchors and being hurled on to the rocks half a cable's length to leeward. In any of the coves where she had found shelter during the previous ten days she would certainly have been destroyed.

On June 10 the weather moderated; but no sooner had they cleared the channel than they found themselves in a heavy, confused sea and once more exposed to gale-force winds and violent squalls. One of these struck the ship with such force that she nearly foundered, and her boats were so badly stove that they were rendered useless. As these were vital both for the prosecution of the survey and for in-shore navigation, Stokes had no choice but to struggle back across the Gulf to Port Otway, the only really secure harbour he knew in the vicinity where the boats could be repaired. So, on the evening of the 12th, *Beagle* was back at her old berth.

As a result of the appalling conditions endured by the crew during the past weeks, the sick list was again causing grave concern, and the surgeon warned that, unless the invalids were given a reasonable chance to recover, many of them might die. So it was decided to prolong the stay at Port Otway beyond the time required to repair the boats. It must have been about this time that Captain Stokes himself suffered a mental collapse; for on June 16 the entries in his journal ceased abruptly. The tension of the last three months, the need for constant vigilance to avert disaster, worry about the lack of progress with the survey, combined with extreme physical fatigue must have pushed his mind beyond its breaking point. Moreover, it is evident from remarks in his journal—such as, "to complete the dreariness and utter desolation of the scene, even the birds seemed to shun its neighbourhood"—that he found the whole environment repellent, and this may well have helped to induce a state of manic depression.

Beagle remained at Port Otway until June 29 and then sailed southward. Ironically enough, the weather was fine for much of the return voyage, with moderate easterly winds. This enabled Lieut. Skyring, who tacitly assumed charge of the ship, to add a great deal to the survey of the coast. Meanwhile the Captain shut himself in his cabin and remained in a state of complete apathy, showing no interest whatever in the proceedings. On entering the Strait of Magellan, however, he asserted his authority by delaying the progress of the ship at various points on some futile pretext or other. Only when food supplies were nearly exhausted was he at length forced to allow the vessel to be sailed to Port Famine, which she reached on July 27, three days late.

When Captain King went aboard he was shocked by Stokes' sickly appearance and despondent manner; but, knowing nothing of his recent behaviour, it was some days before he began to suspect that the man was mentally ill. Having abandoned his project of a year's sojourn at Port Famine, King's plan now was to proceed with all three vessels up the west coast to Chilöe Island, where there was civilised habitation, before resuming the survey. Stokes' demeanour during the days of preparation alternated between apparent eagerness to set sail again and obvious horror at the prospect of another voyage along that dreaded coast. On August 1 he shot himself. In spells of delirium which ensued he spoke of the many hazards and narrow escapes experienced on his recent cruise. Eleven days later he died.

5 Skyring's Quest

THE sickness and despondency prevailing at Port Famine, the severe hardship recently endured by the crew of *Beagle*, and now the shock of Stokes' suicide, left Captain King no alternative but to suspend further survey work and return as soon as possible to Montevideo. Indeed when the ships sailed on August 16, King himself was the only commissioned officer in *Adventure* fit to be on deck.

He had given the command of *Beagle* to Skyring, pending confirmation of the appointment by the Commander-in-Chief, which he had no reason to doubt. For Skyring had shown himself to be an officer of exceptional quality. On two long and arduous missions he had displayed unflagging tenacity in the prosecution of the survey; he was not only a skilful seaman, he had also the most important attributes of an explorer: patient determination, intense curiosity about unknown lands and a delight in unravelling their secrets. His handling of the delicate situation caused by the collapse of his captain was immaculate: perhaps even more admirable was his loyalty in saying nothing of the lapse when the ship eventually returned to Port Famine. Whatever his feelings about poor Stokes' death, he must have been delighted both by this unexpected promotion, and the prospect of commanding *Beagle* on her future adventures.

After an angry brush with the flagship of the Brazilian squadron blockading the Plata estuary, the three vessels reached Montevideo in September; *Adventure* with only ten men aboard fit for duty. On October 13, when the scurvy sufferers had recovered, King sailed for Rio to procure stores. Before he was ready to return the Commander-in-Chief arrived in his flagship, *Ganges*. To his dismay, Admiral Otway overruled his recommendation regarding the command of *Beagle*, and appointed instead his own flag lieutenant, Lieutenant FitzRoy, who was forthwith promoted to the rank of Captain.

Skyring, who thus reverted to his former post of Assistant Sur-

veyor, was still in Montevideo, so it was some time before he heard
the news. It must have come as a shattering disappointment; but
he acted with characteristic equanimity, never displayed the slightest
rancour, and became and remained on excellent terms with his new
superior.

The appointment of Robert FitzRoy as Captain of *Beagle* was
the second link in the fateful chain. It was a challenging assignment
for a man of twenty-three. As the grandson of the third Duke of
Grafton (and thus a descendant of Charles II) he had lofty connections. But despite this advantage, and his undoubted ability he was
well aware of his remarkable luck in being at the right place at the
right time to get such a chance of distinction so early in his career.
However much Captain King may have regretted Skyring's disappointment, and he certainly felt deeply about it, he had no cause
to complain of the Admiral's choice; for FitzRoy was well endowed
with qualities needed for the task. He was already a fine seaman,
and quick to learn from his mistakes; he was extremely conscientious
and had the power of intense concentration upon the work in hand;
he had initiative, considerable courage and the ability to make
himself both respected and liked by his officers and crew. He also
had a marked scientific bent, which stimulated his interest in many
aspects of his voyages, and was later to win him distinction in other
fields. His chief weakness, which became evident at a later stage,
was his tendency to moodiness which sometimes resulted in fits of
melancholia. An ardent Christian, he was a convinced and somewhat bigoted fundamentalist. Surprisingly, he also had a sense of
humour.

As they were about to sail south from the Plata, the ships were
struck by two storms, known locally as "Pamperos ', of exceptional
force, and all three sustained severe damage which took many weeks
to repair. This maddening setback, following upon the delays in
Montevideo and Rio meant that they did not regain the Strait
until early April 1829. Thus they missed the entire summer season
and were again obliged to operate in the far more rigorous conditions
of winter. While *Beagle* and *Adelaide* made their way to Port Famine,
King in *Adventure* sailed on southward to Cape Horn where he had
a rendezvous with Captain Foster who, in H.M.S. *Chanticleer*, was
engaged in a magnetic and gravity survey. After a month spent in
the Horn archipelago King sailed to Valparaiso and then went to
Santiago to explain to the Government of Chile the purpose of his
operations and to refute a current rumour that the British were
about to take possession of the Island of Chilöe.

Meanwhile, having despatched *Adelaide*, commanded by Lieut. Graves and with Skyring aboard, to survey Magdalen and Barbara Channels, FitzRoy made his own debut on the harsh stage of Fuegan exploration; and an impressive performance it was. His main task was to examine a narrow passage, known as Jerome Channel, running northward from the western section of the Strait. Leaving *Beagle* at Port Gallant, he set out with two open boats, one commanded by himself, the other by Midshipman Stokes.* To save space and weight neither officers nor crew took any clothes except those they wore, a rugged decision considering the conditions they must expect, particularly in winter. In this way they managed to stow four weeks' provisions, which "made the boats rather deep", and on the very first night one of them nearly sank in a heavy sea.

Once in Jerome Channel FitzRoy was overjoyed by his first venture into the unknown. He was enchanted by the beauty of the place, particularly by the luxuriant vegetation flanking the fjord— "the whole shore was like a shrubbery"—, and he expressed his astonishment at the gloomy accounts of the Fuegan coasts given by most voyagers. His delight was infectious for, despite the gruelling toil at the oars, the long, cold nights and perpetual wet, the crews remained in high spirits. For example, on May 9, when bivouacked in heavy rain on ground so swampy that two hours were spent in trying to light a fire, supper was followed by "merry songs". Taking advantage of the tides running through the narrow channel they made good progress and, though on one day they were prevented from moving at all by rain so heavy that they could not see where they were going, they covered some sixty miles in the first five days. Then on May 11, to their astonishment, they emerged into a wide expanse of water, an inland sea stretching away to the eastern horizon. FitzRoy named this, his first major discovery, Otway Water.

On the 13th they were again detained by torrential rain, but as they progressed eastward along the northern shore there was a marked improvement in the weather, while on land there was a sudden transformation from dank forest to the dry pampas of eastern Patagonia. Indeed on the night of the 14th/15th, they suffered the novel hardship of being without water for cooking or drinking. Helped by the prevailing westerly wind, by the evening of the 15th they were approaching a low-lying coastline to the eastward. That night they camped at Donkin Cove† near an inlet which appeared to be the mouth of a large river. But, entering it the next morning,

* No relation of the late Captain.
† Named after the purveyor of their preserved meat!

they found that the water was salt and that there was a strong tide running "up stream". This carried the boats rapidly northward through a deep, tortuous channel until, two hours later, they emerged into another inland sea, similar in many respects to the one they had just left. From a neighbouring hill they looked westward over a great expanse of open water to a range of snow-capped peaks in the far distance. Low country to the northward made FitzRoy think that there might be an opening in that direction. He magnanimously named this second discovery Skyring Water; the channel between became known as FitzRoy Passage.

Three days were spent surveying the neighbouring coasts. During this time strong southwesterly winds and a turbulent sea made FitzRoy decide not to attempt to explore Skyring Water. Moreover he hoped to find a navigable passage from Otway Water to the eastern section of Magellan's Strait; so, on May 20, the boats returned to Donkin Cove and the same morning started sailing along the southward curving coast before a fair breeze. At 2 o'clock, however, it suddenly freshened to something like gale force. There was no possibility of landing, for there was a high surf pounding on the low, rocky shore, which stretched without a break for as far as they could see. Stokes' cutter remained under close reefed sail and soon disappeared from view. FitzRoy's crew in the whale-boat rowing westward into the wind, began a desperate struggle for survival. The boat, already deeply laden, became heavier still from the water shipped. After dark matters became a great deal worse, partly because by then the height of the sea had increased, partly because the men were almost exhausted by five hours continuous rowing, but mainly because of the virtual certainty that sooner or later they would be swamped by an unseen wave. With this in mind, and believing that his men could hardly be expected to hold out much longer, FitzRoy began to consider running the boat ashore; a desperate expedient, for it would almost certainly have been wrecked and at least some of the crew drowned. Before he could start to implement this plan a big wave broke over the boat half filling it with water. They began to bale feverishly expecting to be swamped by the next. At that moment the weather moderated and the sea fell. So sudden and inexplicable was the change that the devout FitzRoy may well have attributed it to divine intervention.

It was 1 a.m., eleven hours after the onset of the storm, when they reached Donkin Cove, so tired and numbed with cold (for it was freezing hard) that they could hardly get out of the boat. Luckily the embers of their morning fire were still burning, and before long they were lying around a warm blaze. Despite his great anxiety about the fate of the cutter, FitzRoy fell asleep. He awoke before dawn to find Stokes standing by him, having just arrived.

FitzRoy was full of praise for the behaviour of his men throughout the crisis; though there is little doubt that his own conduct had much to do with its successful outcome. This incident well illustrates (and scores more could be cited with equal force) the appalling risks—to say nothing of the hardships—involved in these boat journeys among the Fuegan and Patagonian Channels, often far beyond reach of help, where even a small mishap might have fatal consequences. They were necessary, of course, because of the still greater dangers, often the sheer impossibility, of navigating the parent vessels in the more restricted passages which, as in this case, sometimes led to major discoveries.

The boats remained in Donkin Cove for the next three days, on one of which FitzRoy, with four of his men, climbed the Beagle Hills, east of the Channel. This gave him an extensive view over Otway and Skyring Waters and he could distinguish many features along the shores of the Strait. Having seen no sign of an opening eastward from Otway Water, he decided to give up his plan to explore further in that direction. Moreover their provisions were running low, and with the probability of contrary winds for the whole of the return passage, it was high time to leave. However, the lucky chance of an easterly breeze on May 24 gave them a splendid start and, after completing the survey of Jerome Channel they reached its southern exit on the 29th. From there Stokes took the cutter back to Port Gallant, while FitzRoy and his crew crossed the Strait and spent a week, living chiefly off shell-fish, exploring two large unknown fjords on the coast of Santa Ines Island; it was the toughest part of the whole trip. They returned to *Beagle* on June 8, and on the very next day *Adelaide* arrived, Graves and Skyring having done a thoroughly professional job of charting Barbara and Magdalen Channels.

FitzRoy's orders were now to sail direct to Chilöe Island in company with *Adelaide*. He had however been considering another plan, which was to send *Adelaide* under the command of Skyring to survey the interior channels between Cape Tamar, in the Strait of Magellan, to the Gulf of Trinidad, and in particular to search for a passage leading into Skyring Water from the northwest. From the Gulf of Trinidad she would follow *Beagle* to Chilöe. As Captain King's orders had been quite explicit that the two ships should sail in company by the ocean route, FitzRoy had serious misgivings, particularly since he would have to bear full responsibility should any disaster occur; but the plan had such obvious advantages that he decided to pursue it.

Another difficulty arose from sending Skyring in command of *Adelaide* over Graves, her official commander. When the matter was broached, however, he was delighted to find that Graves himself was perfectly agreeable to the arrangement. This was one more example of the remarkable spirit of unselfishness which animated the expedition. The ostensible reason for the change was Skyring's previous experience on the west coast; but FitzRoy may have had the additional motive of compensating him for his cruel disappointment in losing the command of *Beagle*.

The survey of the inner channels, which occupied *Adelaide* during the next ten months, was a brillant achievement. It was mid-winter when she started groping her way through the maze of waterways north of Cape Tamar. Her boats were constantly employed probing ahead to find a way through, charting the coasts and exploring the innumerable inlets, any one of which might provide an alternative passage. Sometimes they were obliged to take the schooner in tow, which meant whole days of heartbreaking labour by their crews to win a few miles' progress. For most of the time the weather was foul with the usual complement of storms accompanied by heavy snow-squalls, when the ship was forced to remain at anchor, sometimes in dangerous situations. Twice she struck rocks; on the second occasion she was held fast for several hours, but luckily escaped without vital damage. In spite of these difficulties and anxieties the work was carried forward with great care and a high degree of accuracy.

On July 30, *Adelaide* reached the northern end of Smyth Channel and on the following day Skyring climbed a mountain from which he had an extensive view westward through Lord Nelson Strait to the Pacific, and southeastward over a wide gulf* studded with large islands. From its position and the lie of the land surrounding it, he thought that there might be a connection between this gulf and Skyring Water. So, on August 4, leaving *Adelaide* moored in Relief Harbour, he set out in a whale boat with the mate, J. Kirke, to try to find it. He took provisions for only one week which, as time was running short, was the most he was prepared to spare for the undertaking.

For three days of strong wind and heavy rain they toiled slowly

---

* Skyring identified this as Sarmiento's *Ancón sin Salida*.

southward through winding and intricate passages. Then the weather improved and on the evening of August 18 (their fifth day), they reached the entrance of a narrow channel leading eastward. From the number of porpoises and seals they found there and the powerful tide running out of the channel, they were convinced that it led to a large body of water beyond. The next morning they set off with a rising tide in high expectation of making an important discovery. It was an exciting passage. In the narrowest part of the channel the current raced through at four knots in whirling eddies: and this was a neap-tide; at spring-tide, Skyring estimated that it would be at least seven knots. (This was the now notorious Kirke Narrow. Though used regularly by ships of up to 8,000 tons, plying to and fro from Puerto Natales, it is a very dangerous place demanding great skill to negotiate.)

Beyond the channel the explorers found themselves in yet another inland sea. Unlike Otway Water, its coasts were deeply indented which prevented their gaining any idea of its extent. Moreover, much as they regretted having to turn back, it was more than time to do so. With only one day's provisions left, already their situation was by no means comfortable; and there was no knowing how long they might be delayed by storms. So, after spending a few hours examining their immediate surroundings, they returned through the channel on the afternoon tide. On the morning of the 10th they made good progress before a fair wind; but at noon it drew right against them and they had a hard struggle to make any headway. On the 11th it rained heavily all day and the wind was so strong and the sea so rough that they were unable to move at all. By this time they were living on shell-fish. On the 12th, though the weather had moderated, the wind was still fresh from the northward which again made the going very heavy. However they managed to gain the shelter of some islands on the western side of the gulf, and rowed on until after dark. Happily, that night the wind veered round to the southwest and on the 13th they made such good progress that they managed to reach *Adelaide* before nightfall—only three days late, and just in time to escape a big storm which prevented the schooner from sailing for another four days.

In some respects the second half of their task was even more exacting than the first; for, once beyond Smyth Channel they found less shelter from the westerly gales. However, the approach of the vernal equinox gave them more daylight hours which accelerated the work, and early in September Skyring had the satisfaction of making a connection with his survey of the previous year. On the

10th, the job done, *Adelaide* sailed out of the Gulf of Trinidad and headed into a northwesterly gale. On the 20th after a tempestuous passage, she reached the little town of San Carlos de Chilöe, where she was greeted by *Adventure* and *Beagle*. Three months had elapsed since she had left Port Famine. In this time, despite all the hardship and danger, none of the crew had suffered either illness or accident.

The battered little schooner, however, was in need of extensive repairs; the hull had been badly damaged by the rocks she had struck, and her mainmast had to be replaced. As there was no timber of the required size within reach, this presented a serious problem until the Governor of the Island, who seems to have been on excellent terms with Captain King, presented him with the town's flagstaff which was admirably suited to the purpose. This generous act caused the Governor much trouble; for it was strongly resented by the townsfolk, who were proud of their flagstaff, and fresh reports were spread (even as far as Peru) that the English were about to take possession of Chilöe, and had removed the spar as a sort of gesture of sovereignty.

Delighted by the success of *Adelaide*'s mission, King renewed Skyring's command of the schooner (Graves was transferred to *Adventure*). This time his orders were to complete the survey of the Gulf of Peñas, then to proceed southwards through Mesier Channel, the long uncharted passage between Wellington Island and the mainland, and finally to make another attempt to find a way through Kirke Narrows to Skyring Water. He sailed from San Carlos on December 8, with instructions to join *Adventure* in April, which gave him about four and a half months to complete his tasks.

Although the delay caused by the repairing of the schooner had given Skyring and his men some rest and relaxation in comparative comfort, even the most stoic can hardly have viewed the prospect before them with much relish, and it must have taken a good deal of courage to face a repetition of the ordeal they had so recently endured. One cheering thought was that, this time, at least the first half of the voyage would be in summer, and although the storms were not likely to be any less severe or the rain any less wetting, it would not be so cold, and the long hours of daylight would diminish the risks of being caught by nightfall in exposed and dangerous situations.

In fact the voyage proved to be no less arduous than the other and more than half as long again. Though *Adelaide* reached Port Otway on December 14, owing to stormy weather and other difficulties the survey of the Gulf of Peñas was not completed until

February 1, 1830. Moreover, during the whole of January Skyring was confined to his bed "with a tedious and obscure disease", which seems to have resulted from a combination of nervous exhaustion and exposure. This meant that the whole of the survey work fell upon Kirke, who made many boat journeys, some of them as much as a week or ten days long, to explore the various channels and rivers. Skyring did not fully recover until the middle of March, and when on February 3, one of his officers died, Kirke had to shoulder much of the responsibility for the schooner as well.

Throughout the long passage through Mesier Channel (five weeks) they were in comparative shelter and rain rather than wind was their main bugbear. On the way, Kirke explored all the fjords running into the mainland, hoping to find one which penetrated right through the Andes. Most of them ended in massive glacier fronts (coming down from the southern ice-cap). When clear of the Channel they were once more exposed to the full fury of the ocean gales, and it was not until the end of March that they reached the neighbourhood of Relief Bay. During the three and a half months since leaving Port Otway they had only met with two small parties of Indians (Alakaluf); this was very remarkable considering that *Adelaide* had covered nearly five hundred miles of coastline and her boats at least twice that distance.

For the second attempt to find a passage through to Skyring Water, they succeeded with much difficulty in taking the schooner to Whale-boat Bay, near the western entrance of Kirke Narrow, where she dropped anchor on April 5. The next day Kirke set out in a boat to explore the Canal of the Mountains, a remarkable fjord running thirty-three miles into the very heart of the Andes. Meanwhile Skyring made a more thorough reconnaissance than had been possible on his previous visit of the unknown land and water beyond the Narrow. He was thrilled by what he saw: to the north and south low, gently undulating country extended as far as he could see, in delightful contrast to the rugged, mountainous terrain to which he had been so long accustomed, while along the shores he found deep, sandy bays which seemed to offer peace and security. Eastward, open water stretched away to the horizon. He became so confident of finding the desired passage that he decided, as soon as Kirke returned, to bring *Adelaide* through the Narrow.

This proved a hazardous operation. Though the tides were kept under close observation for the five days that the vessel remained in Whale-boat Bay, the currents in the Channel were quite unpredictable (at least without far longer study), and it was luck rather than judgement that enabled them to get through unscathed. On the evening of April 11, secure anchorage was found in Easter Bay, ten miles beyond the Channel. The first reconnaissance from there was disappointing, for the open water to the east turned out to be bounded by low-lying land which appeared to be continuous. However, to the right of this, a wide inlet was seen running boldly towards the southeast, and as this seemed to offer their main hope, Skyring set off by boat to explore it, while Kirke went to examine the eastern coast.

Skyring was now desperately anxious to succeed. The discovery of an alternative route to the Pacific, avoiding the tempestuous western half of the Strait, would have been a notable achievement which would bring great distinction to the young officer in his first command. But to this strong incentive was added another, still more pressing. The voyage hitherto had taken considerably longer than he had expected, his men were weakened by continuous hardship and their provisions on the schooner were already dangerously low. Winter had returned with its long, bitter nights. Unless the weather were exceptionally kind it might take many more weeks to reach Port Famine by way of Smyth Channel, and the prospect of facing prolonged storms and difficult navigation with a starving crew was not a pleasant one.

For two days Skyring and his men rowed on through the wide, deep channels; two days of agonising suspense. Their hopes rose as reach followed reach with no diminution in the width of the passage; again and again alarm at the sight of an apparent obstruction was joyously dispelled by finding that it was only an island or bold headland that had blocked their view. Despite the sense of urgency, Skyring insisted upon landing frequently to take bearings needed for the proper survey of the channel.

At noon on the second day they reached a point where the channel made an abrupt turn towards the southwest. There it appeared to become shallower and the surface of the water was broken by many islets. In the late evening they found themselves in a landlocked lagoon with only a narrow opening to the southwest, and they camped that night oppressed by a sense of impending failure. The next morning they rowed up the narrow creek for several miles between densely forested shores until, at eleven o'clock, "all our suspense was removed and all our hopes destroyed; for the enclosing shores formed but a small bay in the S.W., and high land encircled every part without leaving an opening". It was fortunate, perhaps, that Skyring never knew that only two necks of land, neither more than a few hundred yards wide, separated him from his goal; ironical, too, that he never saw the water which still bears his name.

Luckily for the sadly disappointed men their return through Obstruction Sound (which it was then named) was favoured by a fair breeze which spared them much of the labour of rowing, and they arrived back at the schooner on April 16, the same day as Kirke. He, too, had had an abortive cruise, finding nothing along the eastern shore but an extensive bight (Disappointment Bay) surrounded by low land. He had, however, seen a small opening to the northeast which he had not had time to reach; and the following day he was sent back to explore it. For, as Skyring writes in his journal, "situated as we were, we had great reason to be very earnest in the search for a passage; and, I think, that no channel into Skyring Water, however small and intricate, would have been left unattempted in this crisis". Meanwhile he himself spent two days examining the remaining channel to the south (Small Hope Inlet), but without success.

Kirke was away much longer than expected, which raised fresh hopes on the schooner that he had found a promising lead. This, too, was eclipsed when, late on the 21st, he and his crew arrived. The opening had led into a remarkable fjord, not unlike the Canal of the Mountains, which they had followed northward for thirty miles before reaching its end. One happy outcome of the cruise was that they had found vast numbers of black-necked swans and coots in the fjord, and had brought back such a plentiful supply of these birds that, for the time being at least, the food problem was greatly eased. The fjord was dubbed Last Hope Inlet. It is interesting to note that all these poignant names have been retained in Spanish on modern Chilean maps.

Committed now to the long voyage by way of Smyth Channel, it was imperative that they should leave as soon as possible. At first light on the 27th the anchor was weighed and *Adelaide* towed out of Easter Bay. But soon they ran into dense fog, and they were forced to grope their way into Fog Bay, three miles from the Narrow. This was particularly irritating because they were prevented from taking the rare advantage of an easterly breeze. It was noon the following day before visibility had improved enough to allow them to attempt the passage of the Narrow. If this had been alarming on the way in, it was terrifying on the way out.

According to their calculations the tide should have been set westward. The entrance of the channel was partly blocked by two islands forming three straits, of which the most southerly was the widest. They approached it cautiously through slack water, with two boats in front to tow the schooner into mid channel, when suddenly they were swept back by a strong current. Then, still more gingerly, they approached the northern strait; but here they were caught in a violent counter current which drove them, quite out of control, so close to the larger island that, for thirty yards their masts brushed against some overhanging trees. Luckily, this part of the island was steep and plunged straight into deep water, for had the ship touched a rock at the speed she was travelling she would almost certainly have been wrecked. Beyond the larger island she was caught by yet another current which sent her racing back through the very narrow middle strait, spinning as if on a pivot. Fortunately the men in the boats managed to cast off the tow-ropes in time to avoid being dragged into and smashed against the sides of the gyrating schooner.

After this escape, Skyring sent Kirke to a high headland opposite the islands to keep watch for the turn of the tide while he stayed on board outside the entrance. At 4.30 came the signal he was waiting for, and the boats again towed the schooner towards the channel. This time she slipped past the islands on a favourable current; but soon they met a reverse stream, "as if the waters from the sounds were gradually forcing back the tide in the channel". However, they continued to make slow, anxious progress until, at about 8 o'clock, long after dark, they found anchorage near the western entrance of the Narrow.

The luck which had brought them safely through this critical encounter held, and it proved to be their last ordeal. From then on, apart from a few storms, they were blessed with fair winds and reasonable weather for the rest of the way; and, after an incredibly rapid passage through Smyth Channel, they reached Port Famine on May 4. There, to their great joy they found *Adventure* awaiting them. It was nearly five months since they had left San Carlos de Chilöe; five months of almost constant hazard and hardship. In two years Skyring and some of his crew had made no fewer than five such voyages, and although none of the others had been nearly so long as the last, any one of them would, by modern standards, be regarded as an epic of courage and endurance.

6 FitzRoy and the Fuegans

I

MEANWHILE *Beagle* was engaged in her fateful voyage to the south. She sailed from San Carlos de Chilöe on November 18, and a week later anchored in Mercy Bay, under Cape Pillar at the entrance of the Strait of Magellan, where she was detained by bad weather until December 3.

FitzRoy's orders were to survey the Pacific coasts of the Fuegan archipelago, south of Cape Pillar. At first he attempted to carry out the work under sail, but the impossibility of maintaining his position in the open ocean and the bad visibility soon caused him to abandon this plan, and resort to the more tedious method of working with the boats from selected anchorages. The first section of the survey, 130 miles, comprised the western coasts of the two large islands, Desolation and Santa Ines. These were found to be beset by a wide fringe of islets and reefs forming a continuous barrier, much of it quite impenetrable. Of one of his charts, FitzRoy writes, "with all its stars to mark the rocks, looks like a map of part of the heavens, rather than part of the earth." In these circumstances it was impossible, in the time available, to do much more than map the outer islands; much of the main coasts was left uncharted, and the channel separating Desolation and Santa Ines remained undiscovered. However this was a minor consideration, for the chief purpose of the work was to determine, by triangulation and astronomical observation, the positions of the main seaward headlands and to find safe harbours where ships rounding the Horn could seek refuge.

By the middle of January, 1830, *Beagle* reached the vicinity of Fury Bay, where contact was made with Skyring's survey of Barbara Channel. A fortnight later an incident occurred which was to have repercussions out of all proportion to its immediate importance; in fact it forged the third link in the chain of circumstance started by the death of Captain Stokes.

On January 29, while *Beagle* was at anchor near London Island, FitzRoy sent a whale-boat rowed by six seamen under the command of Matthew Murray, the Master, to examine a prominent headland which had been named Cape Desolation by Captain Cook. That evening, just before the onset of a heavy and prolonged storm, they reached a cove close to the Cape, fifteen miles from *Beagle's* anchorage, where they moored the boat and pitched camp on the shore. At 2 o'clock in the morning, because of the storm, Murray sent one of the men to check that the moorings were still secure. When, two hours later, this precaution was repeated, the appalling discovery was made that the boat had vanished. Dawn was just breaking, and the whole party immediately spread out along the shore. No trace of the boat was found, but in another cove a mile away they came upon two Fuegan wigwams, so recently abandoned that the fire was still burning. It was all too obvious that their recent occupants, having seen the party arrive, had stolen the boat.

The loss was serious, for without the whale-boat the survey work would be badly impeded for the rest of the voyage. Also it placed Murray and his men in an unpleasant situation, particularly since the bulk of their provisions, which had been left in the boat, was also gone. For the rest of that day (30th), in heavy wind and rain, they continued their search, though with little hope of success. The following morning they began to construct a craft in which some of them might return to *Beagle* to raise the alarm. Without tools it was a difficult job, made no easier by torrential rain and increasing hunger. By weaving small branches together, covering the thatch with some canvas from their tents and lining it with clay earth, they succeeded in making a contraption that was more like a basket than a boat. Early on February 4, when the storm had abated, three men started to propel the clumsy, leaking craft with improvised paddles across fifteen miles of rough water, with one biscuit each to sustain them. In constant fear of it falling apart, they toiled on throughout the day and most of the following night. At 2 a.m., nearly exhausted and uncertain in the dark of their position, they were fortunate to be guided by the barking of one of the ship's dogs into the cove where *Beagle* lay at anchor.

Hitherto FitzRoy had not been greatly worried by Murray's protracted absence, for such delays were common; but as soon as he heard the news he hastened in another whale-boat to the rescue of the marooned party, taking with him fifteen days' provisions. Despite heavy rain and a squally wind he reached them at 11 o'clock the same morning. Having examined the situation on the spot he

absolved the Master of any blame, and generously admitted that the
disaster would probably have occurred if he himself had been there.
No one, he thought, would have expected to find Fuegans on such
an exposed, sea-beaten island. Luckily the survey instruments had
not been lost, and Murray had used the anxious days of waiting to
fix the position of the Cape.

FitzRoy was determined to make every effort to recover the
missing boat, so as soon as the men had eaten, rescuers and rescued,
eleven in all, set out on the search. In this labyrinth of forest-girt
channels and islands, it must have seemed a forlorn quest; but at
the very first place they went to, a small island two miles away, they
found a wigwam with the boat's mast lying near by. This gave them
great encouragement and suggested the direction the thieves had
taken. Two days later, thirty miles east of Cape Desolation, they
met a native family and, on searching their two canoes, found the
boat's lead line. They took with them the man who had it and,
guided by him, soon reached a cove occupied by several women and
children, an old man and a youth. Here they found a number of
items of the boat's gear which convinced them that the cove was
the resort of the thieves who, they suspected, had gone off in their
prize on a sealing expedition. The Fuegans seemed to be quite
willing to co-operate in its recovery, and the youth needed no per-
suasion to join them as a guide.

Following the direction indicated by the two natives, who were
delighted by the gift of some clothes and red caps, they pulled on
for another four hours when darkness forced them to land. Anxious
to win the good-will of these primitive people, FitzRoy treated the
two men as guests rather than captives and allowed them to sleep
unfettered by the camp fire, though a watch was kept throughout
the night. In spite of this, an hour before daybreak, they managed
to slip away into the forest and escape, taking two tarpaulin coats
which Murray had, very generously in the circumstances, lent them.
Thus deprived of their guides, the boat party returned to the
"thieves resort", but as they approached it the occupants fled into
the forest. For the next four days they continued the search, though
hampered for much of that time by violent gales and blinding
spindrift.

On February 12, they returned to the vicinity of the "resort"
hoping to take the Fuegans by surprise. That evening, after a long,
stealthy search, they located them in a different cove, and the
following morning, armed with pistols, guns, cutlasses and pieces of
rope, they rushed the encampment from two sides. The leading

1 Ferdinand Magellan

2 Sailors hunting penguins in the Strait of Magellan

3 H.M.S. *Beagle* in the Strait of Magellan with Mount Sarmiento behind

4 Indians in their canoes at Button Island, near Woollya, where FitzRoy bought Jemmy Button

5 The Strait of Magellan, looking towards Cape Froward

6 The effect of the prevailing south-west wind

C. M. No XIX.

Tierra del Fuego.

C. Horn & rocks off C. Deceit.

7 Cape Horn and Cape Deceit, as seen by an anonymous passenger in H.M.S. *Beagle*

8 Robert FitzRoy, later promoted to
Vice-Admiral

9 Charles Darwin

Vereker, del.^t

Waterston &.

10 Mount Burney, drawn by C. P. Vereker

11 Glacier front. King describes "an immense glacier, from which, during the night, large masses broke off and fell into the sea with a loud crash, thus explaining the nocturnal noises . . . which at the time were thought to arise from the eruption of volcanoes" (p. 64)

12 Fuegan Indians in
wigwams near Hope
Harbour

13 Yahgan man in
Christmas Sound,
"drawn from nature"
by W. Hodges

14 Ona family on the move. The tribe is now extinct

15 Head of Brookes Bay

16 Glacier front

sailor, jumping across a stream, slipped and fell close to two men and a woman who started to beat out his brains with stones. Seeing his plight, Murray shot at one of the men who staggered back but immediately recovered and started throwing stones from each hand with astonishing force and precision; the first of these struck the Master in the chest, broke his powder-horn and nearly knocked him down. A few seconds later, while in the act of hurling his last missile, the man dropped dead. He was one of the guides who had escaped six days before.

A short struggle ensued, in which the women displayed great physical strength, and resulted in the capture of two men, three women and six children. With the whale-boat grossly overloaded with this human cargo, the party returned to *Beagle*, reaching her two days later.

FitzRoy was very upset that the skirmish had resulted in bloodshed. His anxiety to treat the people kindly was prompted at least as much by humanitarian motives as by political expediency. However he did not blame Murray, whose action had certainly saved the life of the sailor; the man had already received a nasty wound on the temple which nearly destroyed his eye, and another blow would have killed him. On reaching the ship the captives were provided with all the comfort available and soon appeared to be quite content. FitzRoy's intention was to keep them as hostages for the return of his boat on which the success of the voyage so largely depended, or else to induce them to show him where it was.

With this in mind, the Captain and Master set out immediately to make another search taking one man and two women with them. The natives obviously understood the situation and seemed to be quite willing to co-operate. On the first night out, FitzRoy provided them with blankets and allowed them to sleep unfettered by the fire, believing that the maternal instincts of the women, whose children had been left aboard *Beagle*, would be a stronger inducement to remain than any bonds. He was wrong; for, though he himself kept continuous watch, the Fuegans managed to slip away unseen, having first stuffed branches under their blankets to simulate recumbent bodies. After another five days of futile hunting the party returned to the ship on February 23, to find that all the remaining prisoners, except three children, had escaped by swimming ashore during the preceding night.

The search which had lasted nearly three weeks had been a gruelling ordeal for the boat crew: long days of toil at the oars, often pulling against heavy seas; soaked day and night by incessant rain and sleeping on sodden ground, sometimes without even the comfort of a camp fire. Though they had nothing to show for all this struggle and anxiety but the charge of three small children, FitzRoy did not consider the time altogether lost, for his wandering had given him some understanding of the intricate waterways lying between the apparent coastline and the mainland of Tierra del Fuego, and also of the character of the Fuegans.

During the voyage FitzRoy often regretted that there was no one on board who was both free and competent to study the natural history and particularly the geology of the region; and he resolved that if ever he were sent on a similar expedition he would take a naturalist with him.

On February 28, *Beagle* sailed round a conspicuous promontory named York Minster by Cook, and the following day found secure anchorage in March Harbour. FitzRoy decided to remain there long enough for the ship's carpenter to construct a new whale-boat with timber which had been brought from Chilöe. Murray was sent with a fortnight's provisions to continue the exploration of the inner passages. He took with him two of the children to be left with a suitable Fuegan family. The third child, a girl of eight, "almost as broad as she was high", was so happy and so obviously reluctant to leave the ship that it was decided to keep her for a while and teach her English. She was given the name of Fuegia Basket after the contraption in which Murray's men had returned after the theft.

FitzRoy had not yet abandoned hope of finding his stolen whale-boat, and when presently a party of Fuegans visited the ship he induced one of the younger men to come aboard, hoping that he might be persuaded to throw some light on the matter. This new arrival was dubbed York Minster. At first he was sullen, but having been given clothes and enough food to satisfy his enormous appetite, and responding to the charms of little Fuegia Basket—"already a pet on the lower deck"—he became more cheerful and quite willing to remain with them.

A few days later more Fuegans arrived evidently bent on mischief. In driving them off FitzRoy and his men became involved in a sharp skirmish which resulted in a slight wound sustained by one of the sailors and the capture of two canoes. In one of these were some empty beer bottles and part of the lost boat's gear. Encouraged by this discovery they raided some wigwams on a near-by island where they found yet another piece of the boat's equipment. They chased the former occupants, who were seen escaping in two canoes, over-

hauled one of them and, after a hard struggle in the water, managed
to secure a young man. Despite the rough manner of his capture,
however, once aboard the ship, the prisoner responded to the
blandishments of the crew even more readily than York, and thereafter showed no inclination to escape. He was given the plaintive
name of Boat Memory.

On March 14, Murray's party returned having discovered the
western entrance of that remarkable passage later named the Beagle
Channel. They had left the two children with an old woman who
appeared to know them well and was delighted to have them in her
care. A few days later the new boat was finished and on the 31st
Beagle weighed anchor and sailed eastward along the outer coast.

For the next two months the activities of the expedition were
centred around Nassau Bay, a large bight at the southeastern end
of the archipelago. FitzRoy was "sadly grieved" to find that the
inhabitants of this region not only belonged to a different tribe
from that of his three passengers but were apparently their traditional
enemies. "As soon as she saw them Fuegia screamed and hid herself,
while at first the other two were too scared to go near them." FitzRoy
claims that it was mainly this discovery, and the consequent impossibility of landing them among hostile people, that persuaded
him to take the Fuegans to England, there to educate them and
finally to return them to their native land to convert their fellows
to a more civilised mode of life. However he had evidently been
pondering the idea for some time and was probably glad of this
new motive to justify his high-handed action. It was a fantastic
scheme, though in keeping both with FitzRoy's character and with
many ideas current in his time. Meanwhile the Fuegans had become
thoroughly contented with their lot. They were treated with great
consideration and even given preferential treatment in the matter
of food over all on board except the sick.

During April FitzRoy completed the survey of the outer islands.
In the course of this work his party landed on Horn Island and on
the highest point of the famous Cape they drank to the health of
King George IV. Meanwhile Murray, exploring the northern shores
of Nassau Bay, discovered a narrow passage leading to the Beagle
Channel which he followed eastward for forty miles, far enough to
satisfy himself that it connected with the open sea in that direction.
Early in May FitzRoy made a further examination of this important
channel. There, like Murray, he met with large numbers of Fuegans
and found them much more friendly than those they had encountered farther west. Many of them were clothed in skins of guanaco,

an animal resembling the Peruvian llama, which the explorers later
discovered were plentiful on Navarin Island.

One day, while returning from this reconnaissance, the party
stopped to rest at the entrance of Murray Narrow; there they met
some natives eager to exchange their fish for such trinkets as the
seamen had to offer. FitzRoy, acting on impulse, told a boy, aged
about fourteen, to get into his boat, and at the same time offered
the man who was with him (perhaps the boy's father) a large mother-
of-pearl button. The man seemed to be delighted with the bargain
and FitzRoy sailed on through the narrow with his new acquisition
who became known as Jemmy Button. Earlier that day FitzRoy
had, with very great difficulty, persuaded some natives to part
with one of their dogs in exchange for a much coveted knife. Reaching the ship two days later Jemmy was greeted by derisive laughter
from the other three Fuegans; but he met their mockery with
cheerful humour and, though unable to converse with anyone, was
soon on friendly terms with all on board.

By the end of May *Beagle* was in the vicinity of Cape San Diego.
To fix the position of this southeastern corner of Tierra del Fuego
was the last major task of the voyage. Plagued by storms and complex
currents, it cost FitzRoy and his men a fortnight of hazardous work
before it was accomplished and they were free to sail northward
away from this land of tempest. On June 26 they entered the Plata
estuary where they met an American frigate, the first ship they had
seen since leaving Chilöe, eight months before. They reached Rio
on August 2, six weeks late for their rendezvous with *Adventure*.

II

On the long homeward voyage from Rio, FitzRoy had plenty of
time to study his charges. Among other things, he learnt that their
fellow countrymen occasionally indulged in cannibalism (this has
been strenuously denied by later observers) and in "a still more
revolting" practice of eating the oldest women of their own tribes
when food was scarce. In spite of these shocking revelations he was
so impressed by their intelligence and latent ability that he became
increasingly enthusiastic about his plan to educate them and send
them back as ambassadors of Christian civilisation. "Far", he writes,
"very far indeed were three of the number from deserving to be
called savages." The exception to this euphoria was York Minster
who, at that stage at least, "was certainly a displeasing specimen

of uncivilised human nature". For the Fuegans themselves the voyage, with visits to various ports on the way, was an amazing experience, culminating with their first sight of a steamship when entering Falmouth Harbour in mid-October, 1830.

While still at sea FitzRoy addressed a long letter to his commanding officer recounting the circumstances which had led him to take the Fuegans aboard his ship and asking him to solicit Admiralty support for his plan. Captain King acted with such dispatch that within a week of *Beagle*'s arrival at Falmouth a reply was received not only signifying their Lordships' approval of FitzRoy's action but offering him "any facilities" towards maintaining and educating them in England, and their passage home. One wonders if a young officer with less exalted connections would have received such prompt gratification of his wishes. From his original letter it is clear that FitzRoy then intended to keep the Fuegans in England for two or three years. For the success of his experiment it was perhaps a pity that this timetable was not maintained; though such a delay may well have prevented much more important events.

FitzRoy was anxious to protect his charges from contagious disease, so he took them ashore at night and the following day removed them to a farm house in the country where they were to stay until arrangements were made for their education. He had also had them vaccinated several times. In spite of these precautions Boat Memory contracted smallpox, and although he was admitted to the Royal Naval Hospital in Plymouth, he died. This was a heavy blow to FitzRoy who was acutely conscious of his own responsibility for the tragedy.

With the help of the Church Missionary Society he arranged for the other three to be lodged in the house of a schoolmaster in Walthamstow, who also undertook to teach them English and "the plainer truths of Christianity", as well as some practical skills such as animal husbandry and gardening. So, in December, they were taken by their old friend Matthew Murray in a stage coach to London where they arrived thoroughly bemused by this fantastic world. Their most remarkable experience (though it is unlikely that they appreciated its significance) occurred some months later when they were taken by FitzRoy to St. James's Palace to visit King William IV. Queen Adelaide seems to have been much taken by Fuegia Basket and gave her one of her bonnets and a ring.

Meanwhile FitzRoy was engaged in working up the results of his recent surveys, a task which kept him fully occupied until

March 1831, when he began to make enquiries about his immediate future. From his earlier conversations with Captain King he had been led to suppose that the survey of the southern coasts of South America would be continued, and he was disconcerted now to find that their Lordships had no such intention. Moreover their offer to provide the Fuegans with a passage back to their homes seems to have been forgotten.

It may have been this blow and the uncertainty as to his future assignment which induced FitzRoy to curtail the education of his protégés and get them back without delay. For, in June, he made a contract with the owner of a small merchant ship, *John of London*, to take him and the Fuegans and James Bennet, former coxswain of *Beagle*, to Tierra del Fuego as soon as possible. He does not seem to have had any difficulty in obtaining the necessary leave of absence, for the arrangements for the long voyage were made with astonishing speed. These were already completed—even to the purchase of a number of goats, "with which I purposed to stock some of the islands of Tierra del Fuego—when a kind uncle, to whom I had mentioned my plan, went to the Admiralty, and soon afterwards told me that I should be appointed to command the *Chanticleer* to go to Tierra del Fuego." Nevertheless FitzRoy honoured his contract with the owner of *John of London* by paying a large proportion of the whole sum agreed on for the voyage.

Chanticleer, however, was found to be unfit for service, and, on June 27, FitzRoy found himself once more appointed to command *Beagle*. Thus the whole of this complex series of negotiations, cancellations and rearrangements was completed within a single month —a feat that would be scarcely possible with our modern system of communication and bureaucratic manoeuvre.

This sudden decision to re-commission *Beagle* and send her back to Tierra del Fuego kindled the ever-latent scientific zeal of the Admiralty and before long the scope of her new voyage had been enormously expanded. FitzRoy's instructions contained a truly formidable programme of objectives drawn up by the Hydrographer. Though this was largely concerned with the survey of the coasts of South America, it included as a matter of prime importance a series of longitude observation right round the globe. No mention was made of when the vessel was to return but it is doubtful if anyone expected her voyage to last nearly five years.

As soon as he received his new assignment, FitzRoy threw himself into the task of preparation with the fierce energy, single-mindedness and attention to detail which characterised all his work. Determined that no expense should be spared to ensure the success of the expedition he contributed substantially to the cost from his own pocket.

Remembering his old resolve to take a naturalist on any future exploratory voyage, he proposed to Captain Beaufort, the Hydrographer, "that some well-educated and scientific person should be sought" to fulfil the role. Beaufort approved the suggestion and wrote to Professor Peacock of Cambridge, who consulted Professor Henslow, who in turn recommended a young acquaintance of his named Charles Darwin. The fateful chain was complete: the suicide of Captain Stokes, the supercession of Skyring by FitzRoy to the dead man's post, the theft of the whale-boat and the consequent taking of the Fuegan hostages, but for any one of these events, to say nothing of innumerable subsidiary links, it is virtually certain that the second voyage of *Beagle* would never have taken place, and that Darwin would have lived out his life as an obscure country parson.

Scarcely less remarkable was the selection of the young man himself. The son of an affluent country doctor in Shrewsbury, he had been a conspicuously inapt pupil at the local school. From there he had gone to Edinburgh to study medicine and again failed to make the grade. As a last resort his exasperated father sent him to Cambridge as a prelude to taking holy orders. In June 1831, after a thoroughly enjoyable but by no means industrious spell at the University, he managed, somewhat to his own surprise, to scrape through his final examinations with a pass degree. Altogether it was hardly the kind of scholastic career that might have been expected of one of the intellectual giants of history, one who was, like Thomas Aquinas, Abelard or Newton, to revolutionise the philosophic thought of his time.

Darwin had three consuming interests: hunting, shooting and natural history. The last of these hobbies had been with him since childhood, and had received encouragement by one of his tutors at Cambridge, John Henslow, himself a clergyman and a professor of botany. But it seems to have occurred to neither of them during their frequent discussions and country rambles together that the young man might pursue natural history as a profession. However, Henslow must have been impressed with his pupil's enthusiasm for the subject, if not by his academic ability, to have recommended him for the post of naturalist with a highly professional voyage of exploration.

The incredible invitation arrived at the Darwin household towards the end of August, shattering the summer peace of that well ordered establishment. The Doctor, a domineering personality, poured scorn on the project, saying that it was a useless waste of time which would provide his profligate son with just another excuse for vacillation. Charles, on the other hand, when he recovered from his astonishment, was inclined to favour the idea, even though it would mean his missing the partridge shooting which was about to begin. But he made little effort to oppose his father's wishes in the matter, and wrote to Henslow declining the offer. The following day he paid one of his frequent visits to the house of his uncle, Josiah Wedgwood, another forceful character, who persuaded him to reconsider his decision. Indeed he felt so strongly that the young man should not miss this golden opportunity that he went at once to Dr. Darwin and argued him into giving his consent. Thanks to this prompt action, Charles managed to cancel his refusal in time, and on September 5, he went to London to be interviewed by FitzRoy.

The two men could hardly have been more different. Though still only twenty-six, FitzRoy was self-assured to the point of arrogance by reason both of his aristocratic background and of his supreme professional competence; his courage, resolution and initiative had been tested and tempered by long spells of danger, hardship and lonely responsibility; he was a man of inflexible purpose; he had no doubts. At twenty-three, Darwin was something of a dilettante; his sheltered life had been passed in ease and security, his time spent largely in the pursuit of pleasure; apart from his enthusiasm for his hobbies, he had no guiding star; he had no experience whatever outside his narrow middle-class world; he had a marked tendency to hypochondria, which seems to have been a family inheritance. That he was deeply impressed by the quality of his interviewer is hardly surprising; that FitzRoy should have even considered taking him on such a rigorous enterprise is remarkable. Certainly he had grave misgivings about Darwin's ability to withstand the hardships of the voyage, but he seems to have been so charmed by the younger man's ease of manner and his rather naive enthusiasm that he was prepared to accept the risk and, but for the formality of ratification by the Hydrographer, the matter was virtually settled at that first interview. Moreover, though FitzRoy had a genuine interest in the natural sciences, he had a strong ulterior motive in furthering their study. As a fundamentalist, accepting the absolute truth of the Book of Genesis, he naturally believed that the faithful pursuit of any line of scientific enquiry, the correct analysis of any scientific data, must ultimately contribute to the substantiation of this truth. What more fitting ally in this great design could he hope to find than a zealous young naturalist about to take holy orders? For there is no doubt that at that time Darwin himself was quite prepared to share his belief.

During the next four months Darwin must have had many moments of doubt and even of sharp regret at his hasty decision. First there was the long delay in Plymouth when, with nothing to occupy his active mind, he fancied himself the victim of heart disease; then, in December, there were two false starts when the ship was driven back to port by violent gales, which gave him a foretaste of the agony to follow, the utter misery of continuous seasickness during the first few weeks of the voyage. At last, on January 15, 1832, *Beagle* reached the Cape Verde Islands and remained there twenty-three days for FitzRoy to obtain an accurate fix of their position. Only then did Darwin awake to the great adventure before him, and with the awakening began the metamorphosis of his whole being.

It seems that Darwin's genius lay primarily in his immense, his inexhaustible capacity for wonder. Now, and for the next four years he was transported into a series of enchanted worlds full of strange new objects. Nothing was too small, too commonplace, to claim his fascinated attention. He did not have to force himself to observe, for his reaction to all he saw was joyously spontaneous; each new scene was "like a view in the Arabian nights". Free from the restraints of specialisation, his winged imagination soared over the vast field of natural phenomena, nothing was irrelevant, nothing unrelated to the whole. Under the spur of enthusiasm, this rather idle young man became a relentless dynamo of industry; his pampered, untrained physique acquired a tolerance to hardship and fatigue which more than once caused FitzRoy to marvel. It is a curious anomaly that Tierra del Fuego, the prime cause of his access to fame, yielded the least important of his experiences, whereas the Galapagos Islands, a mere incident on the voyage and little noticed in the *Narrative*, produced the nub of his mighty work

Besides the three Fuegans, there was another passenger on board. Certain members of the Church Missionary Society had suggested that two volunteers should accompany them to their homes and remain there to help them to civilise their fellow countrymen. Though the plan was given Admiralty approval, it is hardly surprising that there was no eager rush of applicants. However, one young man, Richard Matthews, came forward and was embarked at Plymouth together with a fantastic assortment of goods, from pick-axes to elegant table crockery, contributed by well-wishers, most of it ludicrously inappropriate. His mission might be regarded as an act of heroism were it likely that he had the slightest inkling of the nature of the undertaking. It is less easy to applaud FitzRoy's action in agreeing to take him; even allowing for his missionary zeal it is hard to imagine how he can have expected a totally inexperienced English youth to survive alone among savages in the appalling conditions of the Horn archipelago. However, he would probably not have hesitated to tackle the job himself in other circumstances.

III

The work on the coasts of Brazil and the Plata estuary occupied *Beagle* for the best part of a year and it was not until mid-December, 1832, that she came within sight of Tierra del Fuego. During that time the Fuegans had behaved well and were on excellent terms with the ship's company. Matthews had continued with their instruction and by now they had no difficulty in making themselves understood in broken English. York Minster had become very attached to Fuegia Basket, still barely twelve, and had announced his intention of marrying her as soon as they got home. He was a jealous swain and, though his general demeanour was much improved, he became sullen and resentful if anyone paid the girl undue attention. Jemmy Button was a great favourite with the crew, among whom he had made several close friends. In London he had become something of a dandy; he continued to take a pride in his appearance and was always well groomed. As they approached their homeland all three became very excited at the prospect of their return.

Beagle rounded Cape Horn on December 22 just before the onset of a strong gale from which she found shelter in San Martin's Cove where, "notwithstanding violent squalls and damp cold weather, we kept our Christmas merrily". Impatient of delay, FitzRoy put to sea again on the 31st as soon as there was a slight improvement. His intention was to land York Minster and Fuegia Basket among their own people in Whale-boat Sound and then to sail eastward through the still unexplored section of the Beagle Channel, to return Jemmy Button to his Tekeenica tribe. (It is not quite clear where he had proposed to put Matthews.) But his plan was frustrated by an appalling storm which raged continuously for the next two weeks, and although the ship reached the longitude of Whale-boat Sound, it was impossible to approach the channels. The climax came on January 13 when the sea had risen to a great height and the little vessel was very nearly overwhelmed by three gigantic rollers. After that things gradually improved and two days later she found sanctuary in Goree Road, southeast of Navarin Island.

Here York Minster announced that he would rather live with Jemmy in Tekeenica country than with his own people. Though surprised, FitzRoy welcomed the suggestion, partly because it simplified the whole operation and partly because he thought it much better that the three "civilised" Fuegans should remain together. On January 18, leaving *Beagle* securely moored in Goree Road, he set out with a party of thirty-four, including Darwin, Matthews and the Fuegans, in four boats. They were bound for Jemmy Button's country near Murray Narrow, and took with them the massive paraphernalia for the establishment of the settlement.

They sailed along the east coast of Navarin Island and, on the 19th, neared Cutfinger Cove, so named because there one of the seamen nearly severed two of his fingers with an axe. It lay at the entrance of "an immense canal, looking like a work of gigantic art" which was the eastern section of the Beagle Channel, discovered by Murray three years before. The following day they met some natives whom York and Jemmy called "bad men", and mocked at their savage appearance—"monkeys, fools, not men," while Fuegia was thoroughly shocked. They appeared completely to have forgotten that they themselves had, not so long ago, been in the same condition of filth and squalor.

All this time the boat party enjoyed one of those rare spells of warm, fine weather which sometimes follow the most violent storms in Tierra del Fuego. The sunlit forest and the distant ice peaks mirrored in the calm, blue water of the Channel made a delightful change from the shattering gales they had lately survived. On the 22nd they camped in a cove near the entrance of Murray Narrow, where, for the first time, they met people of Jemmy's tribe. He greeted them eagerly in his broken English, and appeared so to have forgotten his native tongue that he could hardly understand what they said. Passing through Murray Narrow the next morning they were chased by scores of canoes, each with a column of smoke rising from a fire amidships, while their occupants yelled at the tops of their voices. However, by rowing hard and sailing before a fair breeze they managed to out-distance their pursuers by several miles, and a few hours later reached a spot known as Woollya, in Jemmy's country, where they selected a site for the settlement.

It was an idyllic place, particularly in the warm sunshine. Rising gently from the shore there was a wide area of rich pasture, gay with flowers and watered by clear streams. This was sheltered by low hills covered with "woods of the finest timber trees in the country". As soon as the party had landed, FitzRoy marked out a boundary line, placed sentries along it and set the rest of the seamen to work digging the ground for a vegetable garden and constructing wigwams to accommodate Matthews and his three protégés. The whole procedure was an astonishing act of faith, and the naivety of supposing for one moment that the boundary would be respected and the occupants left unmolested is almost beyond belief. For apart from the normal cupidity of human beings (and these people were as primitive as those of the Neolithic age), the various tribes of the southern archipelago (Yahgan) were constantly in a state of mutal hostility which would certainly be stimulated by the "riches" of the tiny settlement. Furthermore, Jemmy had told FitzRoy of devastating raids made almost annually upon his people by the "Oens-men" inhabiting the mainland of Tierra del Fuego.

More immediate evidence of the problems to be faced was not long delayed. The canoes which had pursued the boats that morning began to arrive and later these were joined by others until eventually there were more than three hundred men around the camp, many of them from some of the more distant tribes. Although they were induced to remain outside the boundary line, and with a few exceptions seemed to be fairly well disposed, they could not be altogether restrained from pilfering and FitzRoy was well aware of the possibility of attack. With this in view he staged an exhibition of target shooting designed to impress the natives with the power of firearms. "At sunset they went away as usual looking very grave and talking earnestly."

Meanwhile, Jemmy's mother, four brothers and two sisters had arrived in a canoe. (His father had died during his absence.) The eagerly awaited reunion was a bitter disappointment. "The old woman hardly looked at him before she hastened away to secure her canoe and hide her property, all she possessed—a basket containing tinder, firestone, paint, etc., and a small bundle of fish. The girls ran off with her without even looking at Jemmy; and the brothers (a man and three boys) stood still, stared, walked up to Jemmy and all round him without uttering a word. Animals when they meet show far more animation than was displayed at this meeting. Jemmy was evidently much mortified, and to add to his confusion and disappointment, as well as my own, he was unable to talk to his brothers, except in broken sentences, in which English predominated." However, relations gradually began to relax, particularly after the family had been given some clothing.

By January 27 the garden had been prepared, the vegetables sown and the wigwams completed. The more valuable articles were buried beneath the floor of Matthew's abode and most of the provisions stowed in a kind of attic. That morning FitzRoy was surprised to see that the natives were preparing to leave in their canoes, and a few hours later they had all gone, including Jemmy's family. The reason for this sudden departure was a mystery, and not even Jemmy could offer an explanation. Though some of his party believed that it was the prelude to an attack, FitzRoy considered it a good opportunity to leave the four permanent occupants of the settlement for a trial period. What the unfortunate Matthews thought of his prospects can only be guessed, and although he seems to have put a brave face on it, this may well have been due to the force of FitzRoy's personality.

That evening the rest of the party left in the four boats and sailed some miles along the coast. During the night FitzRoy became very anxious, as well he might, and his fears were not assuaged by the frank remarks of some of his companions who predicted that they would not again see Matthews alive. So the next morning the boats returned to Woollya where, to his great relief, he found that all was well. Some of the natives had returned peacefully, including one of Jemmy's brothers.

The same day two boats were sent back to *Beagle*, while FitzRoy set out with a party of twelve (including Darwin) in the other two, to explore the western section of the Beagle Channel and complete the survey of Whale-boat Sound. Landing at Shingle Point for the night they met six natives who were decidedly aggressive and obviously had no idea of the effect of fire-arms; so, to avoid a threatened clash, they sailed on to another cove. On the 29th, they reached Devil Island near the point where the Channel divides into two arms. (When FitzRoy had stopped a night here on his previous visit, one of his sailors was terrified by two eyes regarding him from a dark thicket. He was convinced that he had seen the Devil until one of his comrades discharged his gun into the thicket and out fell a magnificent horned owl. The name survives to this day.) Rising above the northern shore there was a lofty mountain, surrounded by immense glaciers, which FitzRoy named Mount Darwin. Probably it was the peak now known as Pico Frances which is the most conspicuous object to be seen from Devil Island. Neither the mountain marked "Monte Darwin" on modern Chilean maps, nor the highest peak of the range (Cordillera Darwin) can be seen from there.

A few miles up the northwest arm of the Channel they landed for a meal on a sandy point opposite a huge precipice of ice. They were cooking their food some two hundred yards from where the boats had been beached, and admiring the glorious contrast between the royal blue of the glacier and the dark green of the surrounding forest, when the whole front of the ice collapsed with a thunderous roar. An instant later a series of huge waves was racing towards them. Luckily, Darwin and two seamen had the presence of mind and the agility to sprint to the boats just in time to prevent them from being swept away, which would have left the party utterly stranded.

The fine weather continued and, sailing on through the unknown channel, FitzRoy was astonished and delighted by the views of the great range to the north, whose extent and grandeur he had not hitherto appreciated. Passing through Darwin Sound the boats reached Whale-boat Sound and, by February 1, Cape Desolation was sighted together with many other familiar objects. On the return journey they passed through the southwest arm of the Beagle Channel and on the 5th they were back at Shingle Point. There they met a large number of natives, elaborately daubed with red and white paint and ornamented with feathers and goose down. They were shocked to see that one of the women was wearing a dress and ribbons which had belonged to Fuegia Basket. This gave them ample cause for anxiety, which was heightened as they passed through Murrary Narrow by the sight of several parties of natives attired in pieces of tartan cloth and white linen. They reached Woollya at noon on the 6th, after an absence of ten days.

The place was a shambles, thronged with natives daubed in their most bizarre patterns and all adorned with fragments of English clothing. They were not in the least alarmed by the arrival of the boats. The precious garden had been trampled and largely destroyed. Matthews was alive and unharmed, but the wretched man had suffered a harrowing ordeal and he clearly thought that he had been lucky to survive. For three days after FitzRoy's departure he had been left in peace, but then many canoes arrived and the trouble began. He had been submitted to humiliating treatment by the men who pulled his hair, shoved him about and held his head to the ground as if in contempt of his puny strength. They demanded everything they saw, and if he demurred they threatened to bash his brains out with rocks. Sometimes, leaving Jemmy to try to protect his hut, he escaped to their wigwams where he was kindly treated by the women, who made room for him by their fires and fed him. The men made no attempt to prevent these visits, being far too absorbed in their looting spree. They did not, however, discover the treasures buried beneath his hut. Jemmy lost most of his property, in the plundering of which his own family took their share. York and Fuegia, on the other hand, were unmolested and lost nothing, which suggested that they were somehow in league with the marauders.

Even FitzRoy was forced to recognise the setback to his cherished hopes. Reprisals were out of the question if only for the sake of his three protégés who were to remain behind. His immediate problem was how to withdraw with the remainder of Matthews' property without provoking an attack. He achieved this by distributing various articles such as axes, saws, gimlets and nails which diverted the natives' attention while his party slipped away in their two boats with Matthews feeling like a man reprieved.

They returned to *Beagle* and continued the survey of that section of the archipelago. On February 14, FitzRoy paid another visit to Woollya, not without grave misgivings. He was relieved and delighted to find that all was quiet and that York, Fuegia and Jemmy, still wearing their English clothes, had settled down contentedly. After his departure there had been a sharp skirmish between Jemmy's tribe and the "bad men", which had resulted in the capture of two women belonging to the former, and one belonging to the latter. Since then they had been left in peace and were now busy building canoes. Jemmy's family had come to live with him; even some of the vegetables had started to sprout in the mutilated garden. This scene of Arcadian felicity encouraged FitzRoy to hope that, after all, his experiment might not prove a failure, that the seeds of Christian civilisation which, at so much trouble and expense, he had planted in the wilderness might yet bear fruit, and that later, Matthews might be able to resume his mission.

For the next year *Beagle* was employed upon her various tasks in the Falkland Islands and along the Atlantic coast of Patagonia, and it was not until March 5, 1834, nearly thirteen months later, that she returned to Woollya. The place was deserted and it was clear that the wigwams had been unoccupied for months. Presently, however, three canoes arrived from a neighbouring island and among their occupants was Jemmy Button. None of the ship's company recognised him and all were appalled by his squalid appearance: his long, matted hair hung over his face and shoulders, his eyes were reddened by woodsmoke and his emaciated body was naked except for a piece of hide about his loins. But he was as cheerful as ever and obviously delighted to see his old friends, for some of whom he brought presents, such as otter skins and spear heads. He had not forgotten his English and he assured them that he was thoroughly content and had no wish whatever to leave his native land again. He and his tribe had ample food—"plenty fruits (berries), plenty birdies, guanaco in snowtime, and too much fish"; what more could he want? Moreover he had acquired a wife whom he had brought with him; but she refused to come aboard while he dined with the Captain and was obviously terrified that he would be taken away in the ship.

York Minster and Fuegia Basket had left for their own land several months before. They had persuaded Jemmy and his mother to come with them for a visit; but at Devil Island, where they met some of their tribe, they robbed their guests of all they possessed and left them to return as best they could. FitzRoy was convinced that York had planned this treachery since the day he had chosen to be landed at Woollya rather than among his own people. The main reason for the desertion of Woollya had been a raid by the dreaded "Oens" nearly a year ago, which had forced Jemmy's tribe to escape to the smaller islands where they felt more secure. Also, Jemmy explained, the elaborate wigwams built by the British sailors were too large, and thus too cold and draughty in winter.

It was a sad end to the experiment. FitzRoy took some comfort in the thought that he had won the friendship of at least one of these strange people, and that some day a shipwrecked seaman might be kindly treated by Jemmy Button's children; "prompted by the traditions they would have heard of men from other lands; and by the idea, however faint, of their duty to God as well as their neighbour."

The next day Jemmy and his family were loaded with gifts by the ship's company; and, after an emotional farewell, *Beagle* sailed away, watched by the little group of savages, among whom was the young man who had once walked the streets of London in genteel finery, who had tasted the sweets of civilisation and had happily exchanged them for a life as starkly primitive as any in the world. If to FitzRoy the choice was incomprehensible, it may seem less strange in our disillusioned age.

7 Missionary Madness

POOR FitzRoy! He deserved better luck. A great navigator and a distinguished scientist, he never lost his deep concern for the welfare of his fellow men. Unfortunately, the superb fortitude which sustained him through years of physical hardship and danger in Fuegan waters was not matched by similar patience in dealing with his superiors, and this was undoubtedly the main cause of the rebuffs suffered in his subsequent career. The acclamation which greeted the publication in 1859 of Darwin's *Origin of Species* and the realisation that he himself, an ardent believer in the literal truth of the Bible, had been the unwitting agent of this monstrous heresy must have been a shattering experience. Though it may not have been the prime reason for his suicide six years later, it certainly contributed to the manic depression which at length overwhelmed him. He lived to see his missionary mantle assumed by another officer of the Royal Navy, and the tragic results which followed must have added to his despair.

The tide of evangelical religion which rose steadily during the first decades of the 19th century to establish the piety and strict moral codes of the Victorian era naturally led to a great outburst of missionary activity. At the same time, empire-building provided both a powerful stimulus and splendid opportunities for spreading the Gospel, while conversely the conversion of the heathen furnished a cogent reason for expanding the Empire. People from all walks of life were engulfed by the flood of religious ardour, sailors not least. If FitzRoy was a zealot, Allen Gardiner was a fanatic.

He was born in 1794 and was thus eleven years older than FitzRoy. Though lacking the latter's aristocratic background he was by no means poorly endowed. In early childhood his heart was set on a life of adventure. At thirteen he entered the Naval College at Portsmouth and joined his first ship little more than two years later. At 20 he distinguished himself in an action off Valparaiso which resulted in the capture of a prize in which he returned home as acting lieutenant. During the following eight years his voyages took

105

him to the Far East, Australia, South Africa, the Pacific and South America. Some time in the latter part of this period he became deeply religious and, from then on, his life was increasingly dedicated to the service of God. Though, writing in August 1822, he states that "a great change has been wrought in my heart" and that hitherto he had been "hastening by rapid strides to the brink of eternal ruin", there is no reason to suppose that his earlier life had been more than usually worldly. It is more likely that "the aggravated sins which must weigh my guilty soul to the lowest hell" were no more serious than what he regarded as a deficiency of religious ardour.

In 1823 he married, and three years later, at thirty-two, he retired from the Navy. He wanted to devote his life and his sufficient means to missionary work, but he was prevented from doing so by the ill-health of his wife until, in 1834, she died leaving him with five children. The same year he sailed to South Africa where he founded the first mission station in Port Natal. A few years later he made an unsuccessful attempt to pursue the same object in New Guinea, and in 1838 he went to South America. In the meantime he had married again, and he took his wife and children with him.

When he had visited Chile as a naval officer he had come to admire the Indians of that country for the heroic defence of their independence, and he had an intense desire to convert these splendid people to Christianity. For three years he travelled extensively among the various tribes from Concepcion to Chilöe, sometimes in areas so remote that they had not been visited by Europeans for half a century or more. Since the War of Independence which started in 1810 and resulted in the establishment of the Republic, relations between the European settlers and the Indians had become much more relaxed than before, and everywhere he met with courtesy from the tribal chiefs; but though he tried in six widely separated areas he could not get them to allow him to remain in their territories. His failure was at least partly due to the determination of the Catholic missionaries to keep these virgin fields to themselves.

Though the *Narrative* of *Beagle*'s voyages had not been published when he sailed for South America, Gardiner must have heard something of FitzRoy's exploits in Tierra del Fuego, for the visit of the four Fuegans to England in 1830 had aroused much public interest. It is not surprising, therefore, that when forced to abandon his cherished hopes to work among the Chilean Indians, he turned his attention to the wild aborigines of Tierra del Fuego. With this in view he sailed with his family from Valparaiso to the Falkland Islands, arriving there on December 23, 1841. In those days the small British settlement at Port Louis consisted of a few scattered cottages, one of which was called Government House, presided over by a Lieutenant of the Royal Navy. Gardiner's plan was to use the place as a base from which to make a reconnaissance of the field and if possible to bring back two or three Fuegans to teach them English so that they could act as interpreters. There can be little doubt as to the origin of this idea.

He had expected that there would be frequent opportunities of travelling between the Falkland Islands and the Strait of Magellan in sealing or whaling vessels; but in this he was disappointed and, after waiting in vain for two months, he chartered a small schooner. "After a fruitless attempt to obtain the confidence of the natives on the north coast of Tierra del Fuego", he sailed on to Oazy Harbour on the north shores of the Strait, where he found a small tribe of Patagonian Indians. These people were somewhat less primitive than the Fuegans. Among them was a North American negro who had deserted from a whaler three years before. He had acquired a good knowledge of the local language, and with his help Gardiner established friendly relations with the chief of the tribe, Wissale, who readily gave his consent to the establishment of a mission.

Believing that at last his patience and tenacity were about to be rewarded, Gardiner returned to the Falkland Islands and thence to England to collect funds and recruit personnel for his mission. But once again he ran into difficulties. He had been relying upon the backing of the Church Missionary Society; but their resources were already overstretched by their far-flung commitments, and they declined to support his project. Undismayed by this set-back he searched for other means and at length, two years later (1844), he formed the Patagonian Mission Society with headquarters in Brighton. Very little money was forthcoming, but he succeeded in engaging a schoolmaster named Robert Hunt to accompany him as a catechist (lay preacher). Together they sailed in a brig bound for the Pacific which, in February 1845, landed them at Oazy Harbour, together with three small huts and supplies for several months. Their high hopes were soon shattered. Wissale, who three years before had been so friendly, was now truculent and even openly hostile. It is not quite clear what had induced this change of heart. A Chilean settlement had recently been formed at Port Famine, and it seemed to Gardiner that once again the sinister influence of Catholic intrigue was at work. Whatever the reason, within a month it became clear even to him that his position was untenable. Luckily, on March 20, an English barque, *Ganges*, from Valparaiso, anchored in Oazy Harbour, and in this vessel he and Hunt returned to England.

Bitter disappointment served only to increase the ardour of this astonishing man. He was more determined than ever to find in South America a field for evangelical missionary work. The newly formed society declined to provide any money for this exploratory work. They had however recruited a Spanish Protestant named Gonzales whom they had intended to send to Oazy Harbour. With him Gardiner sailed for South America on September 23, 1845, barely four months after returning to England. This time his objective was the Gran Chaco, a remote region in the middle of the continent between Bolivia, Argentina and Paraguay, the frontiers of which were largely undemarcated. On February 5, they reached the little port of Cobija in Bolivia (now in Chile), and two days later set off across the Atacama Desert. During the next five months they covered more than a thousand miles, walking and riding, over rugged terrain. For most of that time Gonzales suffered repeated attacks of fever (presumably malaria); and at one point while on a particularly arduous march, Gardiner himself became so ill with fever and dysentery that he nearly died. They became acquainted with many of the local tribes but, though they were well received, they were not allowed to remain with any of them.

In September they went to Chuquisico where, in a personal interview with the President of Bolivia, they asked permission to establish a Protestant mission among the tribes. The plan was strongly opposed by the clergy; but it seems that the Church was out of favour at the time, and after some negotiations the President agreed to a satisfactory compromise. The mission was to be sited near the boundary of "Bolivia proper" under the protection of the Government, while its work was to be conducted among the tribes in the no-man's-land beyond. Delighted by this success, Gardiner returned to England, leaving Gonzales to make such preliminary arrangements as he could. Though the funds needed to start the mission were not immediately forthcoming, the Society sent Miguel Robles, another Spanish Protestant, to Bolivia to help Gonzales to negotiate a suitable site. But while he was on his way, there was a revolution in that country, the President and his Government were replaced by a pro-clerical regime, sanction to found a Protestant mission was withdrawn and the whole scheme collapsed.

Gardiner was now fifty-one, a married man with five children; for nine years he had striven unceasingly to found a mission somewhere —anywhere—in South America; twice success had seemed assured, only to slip from his grasp; a large part of his modest fortune had been squandered in the fruitless endeavour. None of this had the slightest effect upon his resolution. He had already formed plans for a renewed attempt in Tierra del Fuego, this time in the Horn archipelago; there at least he would be "beyond the reach of any antagonistic Papal influence". He travelled all over England and Scotland trying to raise sufficient funds for an expedition, but with meagre results. At length the committee of the Patagonian Mission Society agreed to sponsor a modest project and, on January 7, 1848, eleven months after his return from Bolivia, he sailed from Cardiff in the barque, *Clymene*, which was bound for Peru.

This time he was accompanied by a ship's carpenter named Joseph Erwin and four sailors; and they took with them a decked boat, a whale boat, and a dinghy, two prefabricated huts, some goats and six month's supplies. Their plan was to establish themselves on Staten Island, twenty miles east of Cape Diego, the easterly tip of the main island of Tierra del Fuego, and from there to make sorties to various parts of the archipelago accessible to their boats. When the vessel reached Staten Island on March 15, however, it was found to be impossible to land the party because of a gale, and she proceeded through the Le Maire Strait, to anchor on the 23rd off the east coast of Lennox Island. There she remained for three days while Gardiner and his companions launched their whale-boat, explored the shores of Picton Island near the entrance to the Beagle Channel, and selected a site for their mission station in Banner Cove on its north coast. On the way back they landed on the north shore of Lennox Island and, prevented by raging surf from launching their boat again, were forced to make an exhausting trek through bog and dense forest to reach the bay where *Clymene* lay at anchor.

The vessel then sailed to Banner Cove picking up the whale-boat on the way. Luckily the inlet provided excellent anchorage, and the captain was willing to remain there for several days while the huts were erected and the party settled in. It seemed to be the perfect place for their purpose, well sheltered from the prevailing winds and with plenty of timber at hand; there was also an abundance of fish and large numbers of duck, geese and snipe. The goats were released in the expectation that they would breed and provide an additional supply of fresh meat. Only one factor marred the otherwise agreeable prospect: the very object of their quest—the Fuegans.

At first there were only a few of these people in the cove; but as news of the ship's arrival spread along the coast, more began to appear and there was the prospect of ever increasing numbers to follow. Before long their aggressive behaviour made it clear to Gardiner that he and his five companions would be quite unable to cope with their acquisitive habits, their complete indiscipline and their total disregard for the sanctity of property. It would be impossible to prevent the eventual loss of all his possessions on shore and, unless a constant guard were mounted over the boats, they too would certainly be stolen. "From what I have now seen," he writes, "it is my decided opinion that until the character of the natives has undergone some considerable change, a mission must of necessity be afloat—in other words, a mission vessel moored in the stream, must be substituted for a mission station erected on shore." There was no alternative but to re-embark the party and its massive baggage. On April 1, *Clymene* sailed on for Peru, whence Gardiner and his companions made their slow and costly way back to England.

Gardiner's decision to abandon his project after all the trouble and money it had cost, must have been excruciating. In making it he may well have been influenced by the knowledge of what had happened to Matthews when he was left at Woollya for only ten days. Nevertheless, it showed that he was still capable of practical and objective judgement.

Back in England once more, he resumed his quest for funds with redoubled vigour; for his new plan to return to the Beagle Channel with a 120-ton schooner which could be used as a mobile base and anchored off-shore out of reach of marauding Fuegans, needed considerable financial backing. Though he chose to regard his recent exploit, not as a failure, but as a valuable reconnaissance, it was not so easy to induce others to see it in this light. He appealed in vain to the Church Missionary Society and to the Committee of Foreign Missions of the Church of Scotland. He also went to Herrnhuth in Silesia to lay his project before the Moravian Church which had established missions in Greenland. He had a sympathetic reception and his request for funds was carefully considered; perhaps a bit too carefully, for it was not until eighteen months later that the petition was finally rejected. Meanwhile he lectured throughout Britain, but again the results fell far short of his hopes. In the course of these travels he established a close friendship with the Rev. Packenham Despard, who undertook the secretaryship of the poorly endowed Patagonian Mission Society, and who was later to play a major part in the Fuegan drama.

When at length it became clear that it would be impossible to raise sufficient money for the purchase and manning of a schooner, Gardiner proposed instead to take two launches, 26 by 8½ feet, and two dinghies. Though, not surprisingly, his committee were far from happy about the wisdom of the scheme, he managed, by the sheer force of his enthusiasm, to persuade them to adopt it. But the funds available were not enough even for this modified plan until eventually a Cheltenham lady came to the rescue with a donation of £1,000.

After that Gardiner lost no time in procuring his boats and stores and recruiting six companions. Richard Williams, a surgeon from Staffordshire, abandoned his lucrative practice to join the expedition. John Maidment was chosen upon the recommendation of the YMCA. Joseph Erwin, the ship's carpenter who had been one of the former party, volunteered to go again, expressing his devotion by remarking that "being with Captain Gardiner was like heaven on earth, he was such a man of prayer". Three pious Cornish fishermen, John Pearce, John Badcock and John Bryant completed the little band which sailed from Liverpool on September 7, 1850, in *Ocean Queen*, a barque bound for San Francisco. She reached Banner Cove on December 5.

However one may regard missionary activities, so often misdirected, so often calamitous in their effect upon primitive people, one can hardly fail to admire the courage and steady tenacity with which Gardiner had hitherto pursued his aim. But now an element of madness creeps into his story, which is both pathetic and shocking. Twelve years of frustration and futile endeavour may well have unbalanced his mind; it is less easy to understand how he can have inspired his six companions with the same total disregard for reason, the almost eager acceptance of misfortune, which now characterised his behaviour. It must have been abundantly clear before he left England that when he landed his party at Banner Cove his position would be no better than it had been on the previous occasion, nearly three years before. His two launches, *Speedwell* and *Pioneer*, were no more suited to act as a mobile base than had been the cutter and whale-boat he had had then. Moreover, though the size of his party was increased by one, neither Williams nor Maidment had any experience of boats, so that his seafaring strength was less than before. Indeed it is evident from subsequent events that the boats were woefully undermanned.

Tents were pitched on shore and, with the help of the crew of *Ocean Queen*, a stout log fence was constructed round the camp. Inevitably there followed a repetition of what had happened before. The few natives residing in the cove when the ship arrived were well-behaved; but before long others arrived to join in the fun, and they became more and more aggressive as their numbers increased.

"Their rudeness and pertinacious endeavour to purloin our things at length became so systematic and resolute that it was not possible to retain our position without resorting to force, from which of course we refrained." Moreover, though "force" might have been effective so long as the crew of the barque were there in support, it could certainly not have been sustained by the party alone.

Gardiner then decided upon the following plan of action. As soon as *Ocean Queen* departed, he would sail his two launches westward through the Beagle Channel and Murray Narrow in the hope of finding Jemmy Button and enlisting his help to establish friendly relations with the natives of Picton Island. Should he fail, he proposed "to go still farther west to obtain two or three boys from a different tribe and to retain them for the purpose of learning their language. As a last resort, should we find the difficulties too great, we could easily take three or four lads to Staten Island, or to East Falkland, and after their language had been acquired, resume our position here under more favourable circumstances."

For a man of Gardiner's considerable experience both as navigator and missionary the naivety of the plan is past belief. Even supposing that Jemmy could be found after an interval of sixteen years and persuaded to come, no one with the most cursory acquaintance with FitzRoy's story could possibly expect him to have any influence whatever on the natives of Picton Island. Moreover, the difficulty FitzRoy had experienced in rescuing Matthews, even with a dozen well armed sailors of the Royal Navy behind him, should have been warning enough. It is hard to understand, too, why Gardiner should imagine that he could obtain boys from a tribe still farther west, while the notion that he could *easily* take them in his little boats to Staten Island, or East Falkland suggests that he was living in a world of fantasy.

Ocean Queen remained at Banner Cove for a fortnight. It is remarkable that the captain of a ship bound for San Francisco should have been willing to wait so long in this outlandish place. It may well have been because of his natural reluctance to abandon his former passengers in such an obviously precarious situation, though there is no evidence that he tried to persuade them to change their minds. It should perhaps be explained that the westward passage of the Beagle Channel is an extremely difficult undertaking for a large sailing vessel owing to the prevailing, often violent, westerly winds. This, of course, is why FitzRoy did not attempt it during his early exploration of the region; it also explains the fact that the captain did not offer to take Gardiner's party to Button Island.

As soon as the ship had departed, early on December 19, the launches were prepared for their westward voyage. As they were found to be too heavily laden, part of the stores were brought ashore and buried before they put to sea. *Pioneer*, with Gardiner, Maidment and two of the Cornish fishermen aboard and towing the two dinghies, got clear of the cove and headed for Bloomfield Harbour, a bay on the northern shore of the Channel, which was to be the first stage of their journey. *Speedwell*, however, carrying the other three members of the party, was less fortunate. She was towing a clumsy raft of spare timber, which became entangled in the masses of kelp lining the rocks at the mouth of the cove. For four hours she was in constant danger of destruction by the breakers before her crew were able to cut her free and return to the safety of their former anchorage. Meanwhile Gardiner's party were having a rough passage, and although they succeeded in reaching their destination, they lost both the dinghies on the way. The following day they returned to Banner Cove to see what had happened to their companions.

The second attempt to reach Bloomfield Harbour was a repetition of the first, except that this time it was *Speedwell* that got there and was obliged to return, her consort having been driven ashore on Picton Island. After that they remained for nine days in Banner Cove unmolested. It was only then, apparently, that they made the shattering discovery that almost their entire supply of powder and shot had been left aboard *Ocean Queen*; which meant that they could not obtain the supplies of wildfowl they had counted on as their main source of food. They found, too, that fish was a great deal more scarce than they had expected.

On January 4, 1851, several parties of Fuegans arrived, evidently intent upon mischief; so they put to sea once more. This time a strong northwesterly wind drove them southward to Lennox Island where, while landing in heavy surf, both boats were badly damaged. They remained there a fortnight while the necessary repairs were completed. By then, it seems, Gardiner had made his fatal decision to abandon his attempt to reach Button Island and to proceed instead to Spaniard Harbour on the mainland of Tierra del Fuego, some forty miles to the east, and there to await rescue. They reached it on January 24, and moored the boats in Earnest Cove near the mouth of Cook's River.

A week later, *Pioneer* was driven on to a rock in a storm and broke in half. Her bow section was dragged ashore to provide shelter for some of the party, while *Speedwell* was anchored in Cook's River a mile and a half away. So far, living conditions were by no means hard, though malnutrition began to undermine the health of the party, and early in March, Dr. Williams and John Badcock already had the first symptoms of scurvy. On the 18th, the whole party set off in *Speedwell* back to Banner Cove to retrieve the casks of salt beef and biscuit which had been buried there in December.

The accomplishment of this long westward voyage along an exposed, ocean-facing coast, indicates that they could, even at this stage, have proceeded an equivalent distance on through the Beagle Channel to Woollya, where they certainly expected to find, and may well have found, friendly natives. It has been suggested, too, that they could have escaped from their predicament by making their way in short stages round Cape San Diego and along the more sheltered Atlantic coast to the Strait of Magellan and thence to the Chilean settlement of Port Famine. Their rejection of both these obvious alternatives can hardly be attributed to lack of courage and resource. It seems rather that they were inspired by a pious resignation, amounting to a kind of spiritual exaltation, which made them determined, even eager, to accept their fate. Certainly they had reason to believe that a relief vessel would eventually arrive, but it could hardly be expected until June at the earliest. Moreover the arrangements which had been made for their relief appear to have been vague and lacking direction.

There are other aspects of the story, too, which are hard to explain. How, for example, at a time when their movements were being eagerly watched by a large number of Fuegans, did they manage to hide their cache of supplies so effectively that it remained untouched for three months? Also, if the natives had been as bent upon mischief as Gardiner supposed, it is surprising that they failed to overwhelm the unarmed missionaries, particularly during their last visit to Banner Cove, when they stayed there for more than a week and actually purchased fish from the Fuegans. During this time they deposited bottles and painted messages on prominent rocks explaining their situation and directing would-be rescuers to Spaniard Harbour. It is clear from the terms used in these messages that they were fully aware of their desperate plight, which makes it all the more remarkable that they did not adopt a dynamic plan to ensure their survival. As it was they sailed back on March 28, and reached Spaniard Harbour the following day.

Gardiner's journal, miraculously preserved in legible condition, provides an almost day by day account of the terrible ordeal of the next five months. The record of each calamity, of every detail of

hideous suffering, is accompanied by a devout expression of gratitude to God for his infinite mercy and love. This attitude of ecstatic
resignation appears to have been shared by the entire party, and
it is difficult to escape the conclusion that it was a major cause of
ensuing tragedy.

With the southern winter fast approaching they resumed their
former positions, with *Speedwell* anchored in the mouth of Cook's
River and two of the party, Gardiner and Maidment, occupying
the shelter provided by the wrecked *Pioneer* on the shore of Earnest
Cove. For a while they were able to supplement their dwindling
stock of food by trapping ducks and netting fish at the mouth of the
river. In spite of this, and a supply of wild celery as an anti-scorbutic,
the health of the party grew steadily worse. This may have been
partly due to inertia, as was evidently the case with the crew of
Adventure at Port Famine in 1829. In any case, their declining strength
and the increasing severity of the weather made it more and more
difficult to obtain food.

Early in June their net was torn to shreds by ice, which meant
that they could no longer catch fish. Gardiner's comment on this
disaster is characteristic: "Thus the Lord has seen fit to render
another means abortive, and doubtless to make His power more
apparent, and to show that all our help is to come from Him." A
few days later Dr. Williams, now largely incapacitated by scurvy,
wrote, "Ah, I am happy day and night. Asleep or awake, hour by
hour, I am happy beyond the poor compass of language to tell. We
have long been without animal food of any kind. Our diet consists
of oatmeal and pease, with rice occasionally; but even of this we
have only a stock to last out the present month." Nevertheless, on
June 13 and 14, ten "fine ducks" were procured with the discharge
of two shots, "so thick were the fowl settled on the water near the
boat".

Two weeks later exceptionally high tides flooded the camp in
Earnest Cove. In spite of this and the increasing difficulty of com-
municating with their colleagues in Cook's River, Gardiner and
Maidment continued to reside there. On June 28, Badcock, one of
the Cornish fishermen, died of scurvy, and Erwin and Bryant
succumbed nearly two months later. By the end of August the
tragedy was nearing its climax. Williams and Pearce, the only
survivors in *Speedwell*, were unable to rise from their beds, and
Gardiner himself was extremely weak. On the 29th, supported by
Maidment, he made a belated attempt to join the others; but he
broke down before reaching the end of the beach and was forced

to return to the shelter, which he could not leave again. Maidment was now left with the crushing task of ministering to the needs of his three remaining companions, separated by a mile and a half of difficult terrain.

The last entry in Gardiner's journal, as copious as ever, is dated September 6. He was alone; for, three days before, his heroic companion had gone out in search of food and had not returned.

Towards the end of September, Captain Smyley left Montevideo in a merchant schooner with instruction to bring help to Gardiner's party. He reached Banner Cove on October 21, where he found the messages left in March, and proceeded immediately to Spaniard Harbour. It was blowing a gale when he anchored at the mouth of Cook's River and went ashore. There he found *Speedwell*, now almost a complete wreck, with one body inside and two more on the beach which was strewn with books, papers, medicine, clothing and tools. He was unable to make more than a cursory examination before the increasing violence of the storm forced him to put to sea; but from some papers he retrieved he realised the completeness of the disaster. In his report Smyley wrote, "I have never found in my life such Christian fortitude, such patience and bearing as in these unfortunate men." But he also expressed surprise that Gardiner had not sailed his boat to the Falkland Islands, Port Famine or the coast of Patagonia; adding, "I have done more than this in a whale-boat at different times." It was not until three months later that the bodies of Gardiner and Maidment were found by the crew of H.M.S. *Dido* which had been sent from the Falkland Islands with similar orders. Still unaware of Smyley's discovery, they had gone first to Banner Cove where they, too, had found the painted messages.

When, in April, 1852, news of the calamity reached Britain, the harrowing story was given wide publicity and roused strong but conflicting emotions. Some deplored the "unutterable folly" of the enterprise, and *The Times* in a leading article went so far as to demand that no more be heard of Patagonian missions. On the other hand there were many pious souls who were deeply moved by the selfless devotion of the victims and anxious that their sacrifice should not be in vain. The Rev. Packenham Despard was not slow to exploit their enthusiasm and before long he and the Patagonian Mission Society had raised sufficient funds to build and man a two-masted schooner of 88 tons, which was to be devoted to the task of spreading the Gospel amongst the Fuegans.

Thus Gardiner's cherished project, which years of tireless work had failed to promote, was realised as a direct result of his death. From several entries in his journal, written while languishing on the frozen shore of Earnest Cove, there is little doubt that he anticipated this result. It is possible that it was at least part of the reason for his seemingly deliberate martyrdom.

The mission schooner, *Allen Gardiner*, with Captain Parker Snow in command, sailed from Bristol on October 24, 1859. Her crew consisted of two mates, four seamen, a Hindu cook, and a cabin boy; also on board were the Captain's wife, a catechist named Garland Phillips, a surgeon (Ellis), a carpenter and a mason. Their instructions were first to establish a mission station on Keppel, an uninhabited island in the Falkland archipelago (to be purchased from the Crown for eight shillings an acre), then to proceed to Woollya to contact Jemmy Button and bring him and other Fuegans back to the station. It had been intended to include in the party a clergyman who would take charge of the mission station. But as a suitable man was not immediately available, it was decided that he should be sent later to Montevideo and fetched from there by the schooner.

Parker Snow was a dynamic character. At thirty-seven he had already had a fantastic variety of adventures in many lands and in situations as widely different as beachcomber in Australia and amanuensis to Lord Macaulay. Shortly before his current appointment he had taken a prominent part in one of the many voyages in search of the lost Arctic explorer, Sir John Franklin. Though he was a religious man and keenly interested in the purpose of the mission he was not a happy choice. As an efficient seaman and a man of exceptionally wide experience he was intolerant of what he considered the totally impractical ideas both of his employers and his colleagues. Inevitably this led to a series of clashes which eventually resulted in a disastrous breach.

At the outset he was angered by the Mission Society's insistence that only devout Christians should be engaged as members of the crew (the cook seems to have been excused this qualification). In those days it was never easy to recruit suitable men for a voyage of this kind, particularly in wartime (Crimea); this further restriction added enormously to his task and eventually forced him to accept men he would not otherwise have taken. On the three months voyage to Keppel Island he was often maddened by the "arrogant piety" of his senior colleagues, particularly when they insisted upon holding services at the very time when all hands were urgently needed to manage the ship. On a subsequent visit to Montevideo the two mates refused duty because, owing to pressure of work, he had cancelled the usual evening service. He treated the matter as an act of mutiny and, after securing the aid of the captain of a French frigate anchored in the harbour, he dismissed the offenders. Luckily, the British Consul was able to find replacements.

The establishment of the mission station was fraught with unexpected difficulty mainly due (according to Snow) to the ineptitude of Phillips and Ellis, who were supposed to be in charge of all matters not directly concerned with the ship but who were evidently quite incapable of reaching the smallest decision without the help of the Captain. Soon after their arrival, a bush fire, carelessly started by one of the crew, swept the island from end to end and they were only just able to evacuate their building materials and stores in time to escape a major disaster.

It was not until April that the establishment of the station was sufficiently far advanced for Snow to sail to Montevideo to fetch the clergyman who was supposed to be coming out to take charge of the mission. When he arrived, however, there was no sign of the man nor any instructions from the Society. Having promised the Governor of the Falkland Islands, for a fee of £85, to bring back the official mail without delay, he was obliged to return. In August he repeated the three weeks voyage to Montevideo. There, quite by chance he met the captain of a brig lately arrived from Liverpool who told him that he had taken the expected missionary and his wife aboard his ship, but that, just before he was due to sail, the man had been arrested by the police and taken off. There was still no definite instructions from the Society.

Returning to Keppel Island in mid-September, Snow decided that the time had come to act on his own initiative and sail to Woollya in search of Jemmy Button. The surgeon, the carpenter and the mason were to remain at the station; but he invited Phillips to accompany him on the understanding that "there must be implicit observance of the rules and discipline of the ship, and no more of that extraordinary hallucination of mind evinced on the passage out, when he fancied and taught that religious duties made a man independent of all secular authority in a vessel." Presumably the catechist agreed to these conditions.

On October 11, 1855, nearly a year after leaving England, he set sail for Tierra del Fuego. A week later, after passing through the Strait of Le Maire, he made a reverent pilgrimage into Spaniard

Harbour. The silent shores of Cook's River and Earnest Cove were still strewn with pitiful relics which raised the ghosts of the suffering men. From there he went on to Picton Island where he was enchanted by the tranquil waters of Banner Cove reflecting the green woods and flowering shrubs, and delighted by the friendliness of the natives. On the advice of Captain Sullevan, who had been one of FitzRoy's lieutenants, he attempted to reach Woollya by the southwest route through Nassau Bay, but he was driven back to Picton Island by a southwesterly gale. However this was followed by a fresh easterly wind which enabled him to sail his ship swiftly through the Beagle Channel and Murray Narrow—"a wild, magnificent gorge with all the accompaniments of Arctic grandeur and Alpine beauty."

At 5 o'clock in the evening of November 2, when the schooner was approaching Button Island, several canoes were seen emerging from the densely wooded shore. They appeared to hesitate, and Snow, acting on impulse, hoisted the Union Jack to the masthead. The effect was immediate: two of the canoes came racing towards the ship. As they drew near he hailed them, "Jemmy Button? Jemmy Button?" To his amazement and delight, the answer came from one of the four men in the leading canoe, "Yes, Yes; Jam-mes Button, Jam-mes Button," at the same time pointing to the other craft not far behind. "So extraordinary did those words in English sound from the lips of a native Fuegan . . . that I believe there was no one on board but felt as though struck dumb." Presently the second canoe came alongside with a stout, naked, shaggy-haired figure standing in the stern saying "Jam-mes Button *me*; where's the ladder." It was almost a replica of the scene enacted twenty-one years before.

A moment later he scrambled aboard and was shaking hands with the fascinated ship's company. Despite his now portly figure, he was still recognisable from the description and portrait of him in FitzRoy's *Narrative*: quite naked, his long hair matted at the sides and cropped in front, his eyes reddened by smoke. His first request was to be provided with clothes. The effect was grotesque and Snow described him as like "some huge baboon dressed up for the occasion." He then went to the Captain's cabin to take tea while— another reminder of the past—his young (second) wife hammered with a paddle on the side of the ship and cried plaintively for her husband.

Jemmy remembered a surprising amount of English—indeed he had evidently taught it to several of his friends; but a combination of emotion and lack of practice made it hard for him to impart much coherent information. Snow learnt, however, that his was the first ship to be seen in this part of the archipelago since FitzRoy's final visit in 1834. Jemmy enquired after his English friends whose names he remembered and was eager to recall his experiences in England; but an expression of sadness came over his face when shown a portrait of himself as a young man in European clothes. This seemed to be a favourable opportunity for Snow to broach the main purpose of his visit and to invite Jemmy to return with him to the Falkland Islands, together with some of his friends. The suggestion, however, met with a firm refusal; Jemmy made it quite clear that, whatever nostalgic feelings may have been evoked by the memory of his brief acquaintance with civilisation, he had no wish to repeat the experience. Moreover, it transpired later that none of his companions, old or young, was any more eager than he to embark upon the adventure.

From his writing, it seems that Snow was far ahead of his time in his perception of the evils likely to result from trying to force the trappings of civilisation upon primitive people, particularly those contending with a tough natural environment. Therefore, despite the instructions of his employers, now strongly emphasised by Phillips, he declined to use coercion or trickery to achieve his object. This decision was reinforced by a warning he had received from the Governor on no account to bring the Fuegans back to the Falklands against their wishes.

While Jemmy was taking tea with the Captain and his wife, the crew were dealing with his numerous relations on deck and with scores of other natives in their canoes alongside, all of whom behaved well and departed for the shore at dusk. Before leaving next morning Snow distributed a large number of gifts to Jemmy and his friends and relations. This aroused a clamorous demand for more, and some of the natives on deck, including Jemmy's two brothers, set upon the Captain and tried to divest him of his coat and waistcoat, while others, eager for their share of the loot, began to swarm aboard. In a moment an ugly situation had developed. Luckily the sails were already set and, before matters became quite out of hand, the ship began to move. Terrified of being carried away, the Fuegans abandoned their prey and scrambled over the sides into their canoes. After a further cruise through the channels of the Horn archipelago the schooner returned to the Falkland Islands at the end of November.

For Snow, the next nine months was a time of great frustration and difficulty. On his return to Keppel, the carpenter and the mason demanded to be sent home as they had not been paid, while Phillips and Ellis refused either to countenance another expedition to Tierra del Fuego or to leave the island. The colonial authorities, however, made it quite clear that, since he had brought the two men to Keppel, he would be held personally responsible for anything that might happen to them in his absence. He made two more useless voyages to Montevideo to fetch the man who was supposed to be coming out to take charge of the mission. On the second of these visits he was forced to discharge his original crew, whose contracts to serve for eighteen months had then expired. With considerable difficulty he managed to engage enough replacements to man the vessel, but only on the understanding that they would be relieved after three months from the end of May. Ever since reaching South America he had been extremely short of funds and was only able to manage by using his own meagre resources and the money earned by carrying official mail between the Islands and Montevideo.

At last, on August 30, 1856, nearly two years after *Allen Gardiner* had left Bristol, the missionary arrived at Port Stanley, having sailed there direct from England. He was none other than the Rev. Packenham Despard who, as Secretary of the Patagonian Mission Society, had played a leading part in the despatch of Gardiner's ill-fated expedition, and whom Snow regarded as the man chiefly responsible for the many tribulations he himself had suffered. It is hardly surprising that, from the outset, relations between the two men were strained, and it was not long before there was an open breach. According to Snow, the temporary crew he had engaged in Montevideo demanded their immediate release, since the agreed three months had now passed. Unwilling to wait until another crew had been found, Despard chartered a sloop to take him and his party to Keppel Island. Ten days later he returned to Port Stanley, and although by then Snow had engaged another crew and was ready to sail, Despard dismissed him from the command of the schooner on the grounds that he had *refused* to take him and his party to Keppel; dismissed him, moreover, without pay and without a passage to England for himself and his wife.

At the root of this lamentable affair undoubtedly lay the clash of two powerful personalities: one man seething with long-pent bitterness at what he regarded as the gross mismanagement of the Society and their callous indifference to the welfare of their employees; the other smarting under the imputation of negligence and even of fraudulent self-interest—for Snow was not one to disguise his feelings. Moreover, during his short stay on Keppel Island,

Despard had certainly listened to a storm of complaint from Phillips and Ellis against the Captain, fermented by months of lonely isolation, which probably included his failure to bring the Fuegans back with him.

Whatever the rights and wrongs of the dispute, it was not marked by Christian charity on the part of the missionaries. Snow and his wife were left ashore to fend for themselves, at a time when there was a severe food shortage in Port Stanley. Their plight was relieved only by the friendship and help they received from the inhabitants. By selling nearly all their possessions, they gathered enough money (£45) to buy their passage home. Less than a year later he published an account, in two volumes, of his experiences, which included vitriolic attacks upon the Mission Society. He also sued the Society for wrongful dismissal; but, after nearly three years' litigation, he lost his case, though he won a great deal of public sympathy, including, apparently, that of the judge.

For the next two years Despard was mainly concerned with consolidating the position of the mission colony in Keppel Island, and making it largely self-supporting. It now numbered twenty, including his wife and children, two adopted boys, some herdsmen and artisans. In addition, a new captain and crew for the mission schooner were brought from Montevideo. Among the missionaries who had come out with him was Allen Gardiner Junior, son of the deceased captain and a candidate for ordination, with whom, in April-May 1857, he made a pilgrimage to the scene of the tragedy in Spaniard Harbour.

A year later, June 1858, the schooner was despatched to Woollya with young Allen Gardiner aboard. This time he managed to persuade Jemmy Button to come to Keppel for six months, together with his wife and three children, the oldest a boy of nine. Their arrival at the station was greeted with great rejoicing, which is hardly surprising since it represented the first tangible success of the Patagonian Mission Society in the fourteen years of its chequered career. "Rejoice with me," wrote Mrs. Despard, "for the Lord has seen fit . . . to put it into the mind of these poor benighted Fuegans to trust themselves to our hands."

Thus the "poor benighted" Jemmy once again, after an interval of nearly thirty years, assumed the unwanted role of ambassador-designate of Christian civilisation to his own people. He appeared as promising a pupil as before, polite, cheerful and apparently grateful for the benefits bestowed upon him, while his wife submitted meekly and his children romped with the young Despards. There was only one disappointment: their reluctance to speak their own tongue in the hearing of their hosts, which made it almost impossible for the missionaries to learn it.

Meanwhile, young Allen Gardiner returned to England to be ordained, and in November, a month before the agreed date, Despard himself took his charges back to Woollya. Living aboard the schooner he remained there unmolested for a month while he and the crew built a small house with timber brought from Montevideo. His relations with the natives must have been reasonably cordial, for when he returned to Keppel Island in January 1859, he brought nine of them with him; three men, including Jemmy's brother "Billy", their wives, two boys and a child. It really seemed as though a break-through had been achieved.

The new contingent behaved in an orderly manner, became "decent in their habits", and attended daily worship. One of the boys, Okokko, was a particular favourite among the missionaries because of his industry and his eagerness to learn. However, the conduct of the others cannot have been wholly satisfactory, for when after nine months the time came for them to leave, Despard insisted upon their being thoroughly searched lest they should make off with any mission property; a measure bitterly resented by the Fuegans. For the return journey they were placed in the charge of Garland Phillips, the catechist who had been such a thorn in the flesh for Captain Snow.

The schooner sailed on October 11, 1859, and reached Woollya on November 1. Before they were allowed to go ashore, the nine Fuegans were subjected to another search. They resisted strenuously, and eventually, in a fury of indignation, they tore off all the clothes they had been given and, leaving them on deck, scrambled naked into some canoes alongside. The search, though undiplomatic, was not altogether unjustified, for it revealed several items of stolen property.

Captain Fell, commander of the schooner (the second since Snow's departure), had orders to remain at Woollya for a week or so to give Phillips, who had accompanied Despard on the previous visit, a chance to make further contact with the natives. As usual the ship's arrival attracted many visitors from neighbouring coves and islands. Among them was Jemmy Button who appears to have been very angry when he found that no present had been brought for him.

November 6 was a Sunday. Phillips, Fell, the two mates and four seamen, in fact the entire ship's company except Alfred Coles, the cook, went ashore to hold a service in the newly built house. No one seems to have suspected that any animosity had been aroused among the natives, many of whom were on the shore. As soon as the last of the sailors had entered the house, Coles was alarmed to see some of the Fuegans run down to the boats and remove the oars, while others rushed into the house. Then he heard the sound of tumult and a moment later he saw his shipmates struggling out of the building to be clubbed or stoned to death as they emerged. Only one seaman managed to reach the shore, but he too was killed before he could get into a boat.

Somehow Coles managed to get ashore and hide in the forest—perhaps his presence on the ship had not been noticed. Some time later he was found by some Fuegans who stripped him of all his clothes. For several days he suffered severely from exposure and hunger, but eventually he met some relations of Jemmy Button who befriended him until the arrival, some three months later, of the schooner, *Nancy*, which had been sent to search for the missing party. Curiously enough, her commander was Captain Smyley who, eight years before, had discovered the bodies of Williams and his companions in Cook's River.

The cause of the massacre was never satisfactorily established since virtually the only evidence of what actually happened came from the statement of Coles whose terror at the time of the killing and subsequent ordeal may well have distorted his memory. The most likely explanation seems to have been the anger aroused by the searching of the nine Fuegans. The part, if any, that Jemmy Button played in the affair is equally uncertain. Coles believed that he was definitely implicated and that he was motivated by jealousy because he had not received the presents he had expected. He did not see Jemmy during the brief period of the massacre, but he said he was certain that he saw Phillips killed by "Billy". Only one of the Fuegans showed any sign of distress at the massacre; he was the boy, Okokko, who ran to and fro screaming. The cook also asserted that the men who later stole his clothes told him that Jemmy had taken part in the killing and had afterwards gone on board the mission schooner (which Smyley had found at anchor but stripped of all movable objects) and slept in the captain's cabin. But in view both of the circumstances and of the language difficulty it is a little hard to credit this statement.

Perhaps in Jemmy's favour was the fact that, shortly after Smyley's arrival at Woollya, he "impudently" came aboard and (probably against his will) was taken back to Port Stanley. His statement to the authorities there was largely incoherent, except for his denial that he had instigated the massacre, for which, as usual, he blamed the "bad men" of another tribe. Whether or not this was true, the affair was so carefully planned and effectively executed that it is hard to understand how he can have been totally unaware of the plot. He also gave his questioners to understand that neither he nor any of his companions had wanted to be taken to Keppel Island in the first place.

The Rev. Packenham Despard refused to give evidence at the official enquiry into the tragedy, which did nothing to improve the already strained relations between the mission and the Colonial authorities. In his report, the Governor stated that in his opinion the main cause of the disaster was the missionaries' treatment of the Fuegans.

When Captain Smyley returned to Woollya to retrieve the mission schooner he took Jemmy Button back to his home; and thereafter the poor man was spared any further attempts to induce him to change his way of life.

8 Thomas Bridges founds Ushuaia

AMONG those whom the Rev. Packenham Despard had brought to Keppel Island in 1856 was his adopted son, Thomas Bridges, then a lad of thirteen. Because of his youth he probably became more closely associated with the Yahgans who stayed at the mission station than did his foster parents; particularly as the Fuegan children were his playmates. With the natural aptitude of the young for picking up languages combined with an unusually quick ear, it was not long before he was able to converse with such fluency that he was often called upon to act as interpreter. When, in October 1859, Garland Phillips took the second party back to Woollya he was most anxious to accompany them. In view of the fact that he was then sixteen and of his unique knowledge of the language it is strange, perhaps, that he was not allowed to do so. It is just possible that he might have averted the disaster.

The massacre was a shattering blow to Despard and, for all his determination, it is not surprising that he advised his Society to abandon further attempts to establish a mission in Tierra del Fuego, and asked to be relieved of his post. It was more than two years before he received their agreement to his suggestions, and it is possible that in that time he may have gained some measure of sympathy for the unfortunate Captain Snow. When at last permission arrived, he sailed for home in the mission schooner, accompanied by nearly all the people he had brought from England. The sole exception was his adopted son who persuaded Despard to leave him on Keppel Island to look after the mission station.

Thomas Bridges was then eighteen. Though as an infant he had been abandoned by his parents, he had already acquired a degree of serenity and quiet self-confidence rare even among mature people of the most secure background. He had, of course, been brought up with strong religious beliefs; but preaching the Gospel to primitive people was not the only, nor even the main, force to motivate his

126

actions. Close association had given him a liking for the strange canoe Indians of the Horn archipelago, and he longed to explore their wild lands of which he had heard so much.

For more than a year after Despard's departure, almost his only companions were Okokko (who had displayed such distress at the Woollya massacre) and his wife. With them as tutors he set himself the task not only of perfecting his ability to speak their language but of unravelling its intricate grammar. He also started to compile a Yahgan dictionary, a work which took him many years to complete. Thus, by the time the Rev. W. H. Stirling arrived at Keppel to take charge of the mission station, he had achieved a mastery of the language which no white man had hitherto attempted.

It may have been this which induced the new superintendent to reverse the recommendation of his predecessor and to examine once again the possibility of establishing a mission in the southern archipelago. With this in view, towards the end of 1863, he and Bridges sailed to the Beagle Channel in the mission schooner. For the young man it was a momentous occasion. For seven years he had lived on a bleak, treeless island in the Falklands, dreaming of the mysterious world of forests and channels and mountains beyond the southwestern horizon; now at last he had the chance to see it for himself. He found the reality even more exciting than the dream.

Four years had elapsed since the Woollya Massacre. Probably the Fuegans had been expecting reprisals, for it was noticed that when they approached the schooner in their canoes they did so with unwonted caution. On each occasion, however, their obvious astonishment at being addressed fluently by a white man in their own tongue was followed by expressions of hilarious delight. Alone in the ship's dinghy, Bridges visited several Yahgan encampments along the coast; always his ability to converse evoked a friendly response. In the neighbourhood of the Murray Narrow the Yahgans had greatly declined in numbers due, apparently, to a virulent epidemic. Jemmy Button, however, was still alive and in good heart.

During the next five years Bridges made frequent voyages to the Beagle Channel. He persuaded a small number of Yahgans to settle as farmers at Laiwaia, near the entrance to the Murray Narrow, supplied them with goats, potatoes, seeds and the necessary implements, and helped them to build fences. His old friend Okokko was left there to supervise the undertaking. His main purpose, however, was to select a suitable site for a mission station. He considered that Laiwaia was both too restricted and too difficult of access for the purpose, and having explored the whole of the eastern section of the Channel he chose a spot in a large bay on the northern shore, opposite the Narrow. Known to the Yahgans as Ushuaia (meaning "Inner harbour to the westward"), it had a sheltered harbour and was surrounded by an expanse of open country fit for cultivation.

In 1868 he was recalled to England to take Holy Orders, and it was left to Stirling to found the settlement at Ushuaia. Erecting a prefabricated, three-roomed shack (20 by 10 feet) on the shore, he lived there for six months with a Yahgan couple who had been with him on Keppel for some years. With the friendly relations established by his subordinate he was able to recruit a number of local people to help him with clearing the land and other preliminary tasks. Nevertheless, when the mission schooner arrived to fetch him back, one of her Yahgan crew expressed great surprise at finding him still alive. On his return to Port Stanley he learnt that he had been appointed Bishop of Falkland Islands, a diocese which embraced the whole of South America.

Thomas Bridges was twenty-five when he returned to England after an absence of twelve years, a period which had encompassed the whole of his adolescent and adult life. After such an experience, most people would have felt ill at ease in urban society, and it is perhaps an indication of his unusual character that, within a few months of his arrival, he embarked upon an extensive lecture tour. A member of his audience in Bristol was a young woman of his own age, Mary Varder, from the little Devonshire village of Harberton. She was fascinated by his account of the Horn archipelago and of the wild people who lived there, and after the lecture she asked him to tell her more. They fell in love and a few weeks later, on August 7, 1869, they were married in Harberton. On August 9 they sailed for the Falkland Islands. Mary was under no illusion: she was well aware of the privations, the anxiety and the loneliness she would be called upon to endure.

The young couple reached Keppel Island in October. The mission station and the ranch had been left in the charge of a farm bailiff named William Bartlett and his wife. Shortly afterwards they were joined by John Lawrence, a market gardener, and James Lewis, a carpenter, also accompanied by their wives. The presence of this small community made it possible for Bridges to leave his wife on the Island while, during the next two years, he made four journeys to Ushuaia to prepare the place for its future settlement. On one of these trips he was away for five months. He found the house and fences built by Stirling still standing and that the few Yahgan families who had been introduced to agriculture had not been molested. But at Laiwaia the situation was very different. The farmers there had been plundered, and their fields and houses destroyed by jealous neighbours, some of them had been killed, but Okokko had escaped across the Beagle Channel to Ushuaia. It was a sinister reminder of the past.

With the help of Lewis, the carpenter, Bridges built a second and much larger house, extended the area of cultivation and established a flock of sheep. They also cut large numbers of posts for sale in the Falkland Islands where they were much in demand. On each of her return voyages the schooner carried a full cargo of these, which helped to defray the running costs.

By the middle of 1871 the preparations were complete, and on August 17 Mary Bridges sailed from Keppel with her husband and their eight-month old daughter. Mary was a bad sailor and had suffered a great deal from seasickness on the voyage to the Falklands; between Keppel Island and the Beagle Channel she had a foretaste of Fuegan weather which might have quelled the spirit of an experienced seaman. After battling for eight days against a westerly gale, Cape San Diego, the easternmost point of the main island of Tierra del Fuego, was sighted. It was then that the real storm began, and for the next four weeks the 88-ton schooner struggled for survival against the monstrous sea and the notorious tide-rip of the Strait of Le Maire, through which she passed four times. Not until September 27, forty-one days after leaving Keppel, did she reach the sanctuary of Banner Cove, Picton Island. That evening, when the exhausted crew had retired to rest, Thomas and Mary Bridges were alone on deck gazing over the quiet water of the lagoon to the twilit forest beyond. Almost too weak to stand, she clung to her husband's arm and whispered, "Dearest, you have brought me to this country, and here I must remain; for I can never, never face that voyage again".

Four days later they reached Ushuaia. Walking along the rough track leading through thorn scrub to the barely-completed bungalow at the top of the hill, Mary Bridges received the first impressions of this land where she was to spend the greater part of her long life. They can have afforded little comfort. Scattered over the low ground near the shore were wigwams made of branches and turf, which exuded a stench of smoke, rancid butter and refuse flung close outside. Around the hovels dark figures, some partly clothed in otter-skins, others almost naked, stood or squatted, gazing intently at the new arrivals. Though it was already mid-spring a raw wind blew down from the mountains; snow lay in patches on the open ground about the settlement, while in the surrounding forest and on the bare hills above the treeline it was deep and unbroken. Perhaps she hoped that one day she might become reconciled to this alien world; she can hardly have imagined that she would grow to love it in all its moods.

Although she had a certain amount of company—the Lewises and later the Lawrences—by far the most daunting aspect of her situation was the isolation. The nearest white community was the Chilean convict settlement at Punta Arenas, a hundred and twenty miles away over a range of mountains and across the Magellan Strait. Though these mountains are not high, it was not until twenty years later that anyone succeeded in crossing the main island from the Beagle Channel to its northern shores. This was partly due to the difficult terrain but mainly because the country between was inhabited by the Ona, a fiercely hostile tribe. Thus, for many years, the only means of contact with the outside world was the mission schooner which came from the Falkland Islands, on an average, twice a year. Apart from this, in whatever emergency that might arise the tiny community had to rely entirely upon their own courage and resource.

Although Thomas Bridges, by his mastery of the Yahgan language, had succeeded where all others had failed in establishing a peaceful relationship with the natives of the Beagle Channel, a great deal more was required to ensure its continuance. Even if he had chosen to forget the grim record of the past, he could not ignore the unpredictability of these people, their sudden outbreaks of violence and their long-standing feuds. Their quarrels were usually caused by jealousy over women, but often they were over some quite trivial matter; even a sharp word to a child might be regarded as a gross insult to its parent and so provoke a strong reaction. When fights occurred they were either conducted with bare hands or large stones were used, not for throwing, but for striking at an opponent's head. Though premeditated murder seems to have been rare among the Yahgan, these contests sometimes resulted in the death of one of the protagonists. The relations of the victim would then seek vengeance; and if he happened to belong to a group from a neighbouring island the affair might well result in a canoe-borne invasion. Bridges was constantly trying to settle these disputes, and whenever he heard of a disturbance he would hasten to intercede between the contestants and to try, not always successfully, to prevent bloodshed. He was never armed on these occasions, though his life was often in danger, and he was careful to avoid using threats of force.

Sometimes he himself was the target of vengeance. On one occasion, for example, he managed to frustrate an attempt by one of the Yahgans to abduct another's wife. The disappointed seducer was so furious that he declared his intention to go to the missionary's house and kill him with a hatchet. Bridges was warned of the plot but was inclined to discount the story as mischievous gossip, until the man appeared at his door with some trivial request. Then he calmly asked the Yahgan to hand over the hatchet concealed beneath his skin cloak. The native was so astonished that he complied without a word. He was still more amazed then the weapon was returned to him with a gentle request that when he called again he might leave it at home.

To make contact with the inhabitants of the remote parts of the archipelago, Bridges undertook long journeys in an open boat alone with a Yahgan crew. Some of these lasted ten days or more, and sometimes his return was long overdue. He had a reputation for reckless daring, but he must have been a thoroughly competent seaman, and it seems that he was never happier than in vile weather. His sons have recalled how, when steering his boat in a violent storm, he would sing at the top of his voice from sheer exuberance. This capacity for tireless delight in every aspect of his wild environment was surely the secret of his success; for it gave him an acute understanding of all its components, which promoted harmony and abolished fear.

The same quality characterised his dealings with the island people and won him their respect and confidence. With this and his mastery of their language it was not long before he had acquired a more intimate knowledge of the mode of life and the customs of the Yahgans than any other white man has ever possessed.

At that time it was estimated that the inhabitants of Tierra del Fuego numbered between seven and nine thousand. They were divided into three distinct tribes: the Ona, who were landsmen living in the interior of the main island, and the Alakaluf and the Yahgan, both of them canoe Indians occupying its southern shores and the outer islands. The western part of the archipelago was the home of the Alakaluf, though their habitat also extended far up the Pacific coast of Patagonia. Brecknock Peninsula (a westerly extension of the great peninsula of the Cordillera Darwin) formed a natural boundary between them and the Yahgans, whose territory extended eastward along the southern coast of the main island and included all the southern islands as far as Cape Horn. They were thus the southernmost inhabitants of the earth. The name "Yahgan" was

invented by Bridges himself; it was an abbreviation of the word
Yahgashagalumoala meaning "People of the Mountain Valley
Channel", which in fact referred only to those living in the neigh-
bourhood of Murray Narrow.

Like the Alakaluf, the Yahgan were semi-nomadic. Though each
group usually confined its activities to a restricted area, they had
no fixed abode and little community life. They spent much of their
time in their canoes, travelling in family units from place to place
in search of food, and they never ventured far inland. Their main
diet consisted of fish, mussels, limpets and sea-urchins. supple-
mented by various fungi, berries and edible plants found in the
forest; but they also killed birds, otters, seals and foxes, while
stranded whales provided them with a valuable supply of oil with
which they smeared their bodies. They had no set meal times, and
ate whenever they felt inclined. Nor did they bother to store their
food since there was nearly always a plentiful supply at hand. Only
on rare occasions, when they were trapped on an exposed shore by
a prolonged storm and were thus prevented from using their canoes,
did they suffer an uncomfortable shortage.

Since, among primitive people, it is the need to survive which
provides the main stimulus to advance, it may well be that this
abundance of readily available food was the chief reason for the
backward state of both the Alakaluf and the Yahgan. Certainly
they displayed great ability in the manufacture of the few implements they used. Their canoes, for example, which won such
extravagant praise from Drake's chaplain, have been described as
among the most delicately constructed and efficient of any such craft
in existence. A frame of split saplings sheathed in strips of nothofagus bark sewn together with whalebone needles and animal sinew,
they "had a sheer at once pleasing to the eye and well adapted to
ride the most tempestuous seas in the world". Their axes, the heads
of which were made from large clam shells, and the harpoons they
used for spearing fish were both cunningly contrived and skilfully
fashioned. Further evidence of their intelligence was the richness
of their language which, according to Bridges, commanded a very
remarkable range and subtlety of expression. His Yahgan dictionar
contained no fewer than 40,000 words.

By contrast, their wigwams were utterly crude. A number of
saplings stuck in the ground enclosed a circle some nine feet in
diameter; these were bent over and intertwined so as to form a
dome-shaped frame which was covered with grass and turf. The
floor was strewn with a deep litter of grass and twigs, and a fire was

kept burning just inside the entrance. The people had no idea of sanitation and were as likely to deposit their excrement close to their wigwams as anywhere else. Prior to their extensive contact with white men, they seem to have been singularly free from disease, and thus had no reason to fear dirt. They had no cooking utensils of any kind; most of their food was either grilled or baked, while some of it was eaten raw.

Considering the hard climate in which they lived, one of the strangest characteristics of the Yahgan was the scantiness of their attire. Most of them wore small skin aprons, presumably to protect rather than hide their genitals. They also had small capes of otter skin draped across their shoulders, though all the children and many of the adults were content to remain entirely naked in summer and winter alike, whatever the weather. They did, however, cover themselves with whale-oil whenever supplies were available. Otherwise they seem to have been largely impervious to cold and damp, which suggests that they had developed a remarkably efficient metabolism. Though the average height of the men was only about five feet two inches, they were very strong, as FitzRoy's sailors had discovered to their cost. The women wore necklaces of polished shells and bones, while the men made a practice of daubing their faces and bodies with charcoal and red and white paint in various bizarre patterns.

The division of work amongst the sexes was clearly defined. The men gathered fuel and vegetables, tended the fires, made and repaired the canoes, hunted otters, seals and birds and speared large fish. Apart from the spear, their main weapon was a sling with which they could throw pebbles with astonishing accuracy and force. It is said that they could kill a sitting duck from a distance of 200 yards, or stun a guanaco 100 yards away. The women did the cooking, paddled the canoes and attended to their mooring; they also caught the smaller fish and dived for shell-fish in deep water. Throughout the archipelago, beaches are comparatively rare, so the canoes were often moored among the dense forests of kelp which grow on reefs fringing the coast and which make excellent break-waters. They flourish in as much as fourteen fathoms of water and the stems of individual plants can attain a length of over two hundred yards, while the mass of leaves floating on the surface is sometimes so thick that it can support the weight of gulls and herons. Besides the security afforded by these kelp forests, they abounded with fish, which provided an additional attraction for the Yahgans. When landing at such places the men were first put ashore with the baggage; the women would then paddle the canoes out to the kelp, secure them to the tough stems and swim back. The last operation required considerable skill to avoid becoming entangled in the weed.

This sharp division of responsibility is well illustrated by the remarkable fact that, though the women were excellent swimmers, it was very rare to find a man who could swim at all. It also suggests that accidents at sea, such as the upsetting of a canoe, were not common. Women would go swimming with their infant daughters on their backs so as to accustom them to the water. In very cold weather, when the floating kelp leaves were coated with frost, the swimmer's task would be complicated by the baby girl climbing on to her head to escape contact with the ice. For all this Spartan upbringing the Yahgan were fond of their children and slow to punish their mischief, though they expected them to fend for themselves at a very early age.

To make fire, the Yahgan used iron pyrites, which was far more effective than flint. As it was only to be found in one locality in the entire archipelago—Mercury Sound on Clarence Island—it was a most valuable commodity, particularly to the people who lived at a great distance from its source. For tinder they used a filmy web found in a certain species of ground fungus, fine bird's down or the nests of insects. In practice, however, they seldom needed fire-stone or tinder, for their fires were kept alight in their wigwams day and night, and while fishing or travelling, smouldering embers were heaped on beds of sand and turf in the centre of the canoes.

The primitive state of the canoe Indians of Tierra del Fuego, their nakedness, the abject discomfort in which they appeared to live, aroused the pity of the more humane among the early explorers. As we have seen, some of these good people went to considerable lengths in their attempts to alleviate the suffering of the "poor, benighted savages". Perhaps all their compassion was misplaced; it may be that in spite of their simplicity—or indeed because of it— the Yahgan and Alakaluf were as happy as any inhabitants of the world. Certainly Jemmy Button, having tasted the delights of civilisation, had no hesitation in rejecting them in favour of his native way of life. Given complete immunity from cold and the necessary skills, it had, indeed, much to recommend it. The people were singularly free from drudgery; they were strangers to heavy, repetitive toil; there was a great variety in their daily occupation, and many of their tasks demanded a high degree of dexterity and cunning—important ingredients in any recipe for human content-ment. There was no government to dictate their actions and no tribal chief to extort tribute; indeed their language contained no word to express the concept of obedience. Though Europeans found their climate harsh, they themselves were superbly adapted to meet the rigours.

In their zeal to improve the lot of backward peoples, the would-be benefactors of the 19th century made two fundamental errors. They judged all conditions of life by their own standards; comfort, cleanliness, habits, codes of behaviour were, in terms of welfare, measured by them against the yardstick of European sensitivity, taste and practice. They were unable to conceive that an Eskimo woman living in an igloo on a diet of raw fish could be as happy as any suburban housewife, or that a Tibetan shepherd might find polyandry more wholesome than monogamy. Secondly, they were blithely unaware of the dangers of interfering with aboriginal tribes and the havoc that could result from forcing or persuading them to adopt alien customs and techniques. The advantage of hindsight and our disenchantment with the benefits of civilisation make us prone to scoff at the mistakes of our forebears and to deplore their arrogant assumption of superiority; but there is little evidence that our present-day idealists are endowed with more wisdom and humility.

By 1876, the settlement at Ushuaia was well established and had grown to the size of a small village. There were then four British families living there and more than one hundred Yahgans had broken with their nomadic habits to take up permanent residence. There was also a fluctuating population of visitors from various parts of the archipelago who were attracted by the hope of trade or by sheer curiosity. Most of them came from neighbouring islands, but about this time a canoe arrived from the rugged coast of the distant Brecknock Peninsula. Among the party was none other than Fuegia Basket who, some forty-five years before, had been taken to England by Captain FitzRoy. She was in excellent health and delighted to recall the fantastic adventure of her childhood. She had forgotten all but a few words of English, though she remembered the names of some of the people she had known in London. She told Bridges that York Minster had been killed in retaliation for a murder he had committed. Her present husband was a youth of eighteen who had come with her. Among the Yahgan it was customary for a young man to marry a middle-aged woman who had the experience and skill to attend to his domestic needs, and to take a young bride when he himself was more mature. Fuegia did not stay long in Ushuaia, for she was evidently pining to return home. Some eight years later, Bridges visited her in her native land.

Thomas and Mary Bridges had three sons and three daughters; the last was born in 1881. The developing settlement was a wonderful environment for the children, and they all acquired a deep and lasting affection for the strange country of their birth. Whatever they may have missed from lack of normal schooling was compensated by a score of benefits denied to the average child raised in civilised surroundings. They had no need for make-believe or artificial stimulus. With limitless wilderness at their back door they soon acquired an intimate knowledge of a wide range of natural history; the unexplored country which lay beyond the nearest hills provided ample range for the imagination. From a very early age, the boys were allowed to go with the Yahgans on their hunting and fishing expeditions; and even before they were eight years old they began to accompany their father on his long boat journeys to distant islands and channels. Self-reliance, endurance, a sense of responsibility and a calm response to critical situations, these were among the earliest lessons they learnt.

From time to time there were other visitors to Ushuaia besides the wandering Yahgan. In 1882, an Italian expedition came to make certain observations in the Beagle Channel. The leader, Captain Bové, persuaded Bridges to join them which he did, together with two of his sons, Despard and Lucas, and two Yahgans from the settlement. Unfortunately, the expedition schooner was wrecked on the coast near Spaniard Harbour. Though the whole party managed to get ashore, it was largely due to the missionary and the two Yahgans that they all survived. A year later, a French scientific expedition arrived in the archipelago and established a base on the southwest coast of Hoste Island, one of the most desolate parts of the region. Despard and Lucas, then aged eleven and nine respectively, spent some time there acting as interpreters between the Frenchmen and the natives and helping the scientists with their practical knowledge of the local flora and fauna.

Other visitors from the outside world were the survivors from various shipwrecks. There was, for example, the German barque on her way from Liverpool to San Francisco with a cargo of coal which caught fire after rounding Cape Horn. The crew of twenty-two abandoned the vessel ten minutes before she blew up. Though far beyond sight of the coast, they had seen from the ship's deck the ice peaks of Tierra del Fuego and the three boats headed in their direction. Though it was mid-winter the weather was calm and clear. They had an up-to-date British Admiralty chart on which there was a reference to the Ushuaia settlement together with directions as to the best way to reach it. But in spite of this, they were unable to find the entrance to the passage leading to Murray Narrow and, concluding that the chart was wrong, they turned and coasted along the southern shores of Navarin Island. Near Picton Island, they were lucky enough to encounter a Yahgan who had had many dealings with the mission station and who willingly piloted them to Ushuaia, which they reached ten days after leaving their ship. A few years before, their chances of survival would have been very remote.

In September 1884, the tranquility of the settlement was disturbed by the unheralded arrival of four ships of the Argentine navy to establish a sub-prefecture at Ushuaia. Hitherto the government of neither Chile nor Argentina had shown any active interest in Tierra del Fuego, though it was understood that the archipelago should be divided between the two countries in a ratio of about two to one respectively. The boundary line was to run straight from a point on the Beagle Channel twelve miles west of Ushuaia to Cape Espíritu Santo at the eastern entrance of the Magellan Strait. The object of the sub-prefecture was simply to confirm national territorial claims by occupation, and the missionaries were assured that there was no intention to interfere with their work. The Argentine flag was hoisted to the accompaniment of a twenty-one-gun salute, and a few weeks later the ships departed leaving the sub-prefect and his staff of twenty-two, which included several British sailors. The following year the establishment was greatly enlarged; Ushuaia was declared the capital of Argentine Tierra del Fuego and a governor was installed. For several decades the ponderous administrative machine served little purpose save that of showing the flag.

Though members of the mission remained on excellent terms with the newcomers, Bridges had been dreading the arrival of large numbers of white men who, by the introduction of alcohol and other subversive influences, would inevitably undermine both the natural simplicity of the Yahgans and the delicate structure of confidence which he had built during the past twelve years. He had already proposed the creation of a kind of native reserve to be supervised by the mission and free from outside interference. The plan, however, was rejected by his committee in London on the ground that an Anglican mission should confine its activities to evangelical work.

The disaster he had feared came more swiftly than he had expected and in a totally different form. Three weeks after the arrival of the Argentine ships an epidemic of measles broke out among the Yahgans at Ushuaia and spread to neighbouring bays and islands. The effect was devastating. Within a few days the people were dying at such a rate that it was impossible to dig graves fast enough. In outlying districts the dead were merely put outside the wigwams or, if the other occupants had the strength, dragged to the nearest bushes. In the initial onslaught of the disease more than half the population of the district perished; the survivors were so weakened that during the next two years fifty per cent of them succumbed, apparently from its after effects. The reason for this terrible calamity is clear: while through the ages Europeans have developed a large measure of immunity from the more serious effects of measles, the Yahgan, for all their phenomenal toughness and resilience, had no such natural protection. Presumably the scourge spread throughout the southern archipelago for, ten years later, it was estimated that there were only three hundred Yahgans alive out of a former population of some three thousand. Today there are none.

Whether or not Thomas Bridges had already become disillusioned about the future value of the Ushuaia mission, the frustration of his plans for the protection of the Yahgan against the contamination of outside influences induced him to resign from his post and attempt to establish a ranch of his own. His decision was badly received by the London committee where he was described as a rat leaving a sinking ship and the view was expressed that his action had "undoubtedly been instigated by the Evil One to his ruin". This was surely a little ungenerous considering his twenty-odd years of devoted and often dangerous service.

For Bridges, it was certainly a bold step, perhaps the most reckless of his adventurous career. Though still in his early forties, he was a sick man. A prodigious worker, he had driven himself relentlessly and had often endured severe hardship and privation, particularly during his long boat journeys. Whether from these or other causes, he had suffered frequent collapse, and in 1879 he had been so ill that he had gone to Punta Arenas for medical advice. A doctor there had diagnosed cancer of the stomach and he was sent to England, where he was told that he had not long to live. However, he chose to ignore the warning and returned to Ushuaia to carry on as before. The only private means he had was the money he had saved from his stipend of £150 a year. Of course he had had valuable experience of creating a ranch in the wilderness; but at Ushuaia he had been supported by his employers in London, and the mission schooner had brought regular supplies from the Falkland Islands. To attempt such a venture on his own and with a young family to rear seemed to most of his friends so hazardous as to be thoroughly irresponsible. There was, however, one notable exception: Captain Willis, the master of the mission schooner, was so confident of the success of the undertaking that he lent him the whole of his savings which amounted to £700.

In July 1886, Bridges went to Buenos Aires to persuade the Argentine Government to make him a grant of land on the northern shores of the Beagle Channel, forty miles east of Ushuaia. He had some reason to expect a favourable response for, at that time, the Government were anxious to encourage settlement among the vast, wild regions in the south of their country. In the capital, he was the guest of Dr. Moreno, a celebrated scientist with whom he had often corresponded about the natural history of the Beagle Channel. His host had many influential friends and it was not long before Bridges obtained an interview with President Roca, one of Argentine's more enlightened statesmen, who offered his full support. As a result, he received a grant of seventy-two square miles of land. It was, of course, several years before the property was surveyed and the title deeds issued, but as there were no competitors in the field, this was a matter of little consequence.

From Buenos Aires Bridges sailed to England where he purchased all he needed to start his ranch, including a large supply of flour and sugar, a South Devon bull, four Romney Marsh rams, a couple of pigs and two sheep dogs. To transport them to the Beagle Channel he managed to charter a large brigantine for the modest charge of fifty shillings a day; but as the voyage took thirty-five and a half weeks it cost him a substantial part of his capital. Later he used the same vessel to carry to the Falkland Islands a full cargo of posts which he exchanged for three hundred sheep and seventy head of cattle.

From his intimate knowledge of the region, Bridges had chosen the site for his ranch with great care. Some forty miles east of Ushuaia, it extended along fourteen miles of the north coast of the Beagle Channel (the actual shoreline was twice that length) and in depth to the crest of the first range of hills, about six miles inland. The property also included a dozen off-shore islands, the largest of which, Gable Island, was five miles long and three miles wide. The place selected for the farmstead was at the head of a deep gulf which provided anchorage for fairly large vessels. It was named Harberton after Mary Bridges' home village in Devon.

Arriving there in April 1887, the family spent the first winter in a one-room shack. The weather throughout was exceptionally severe, with the result that they were fully occupied with the sheer struggle for their own survival and that of their livestock; and it was not until six months later that constructive work could begin— building a house, clearing scrub and forest for grazing land, digging, planting and fencing. A number of Yahgans migrated to Harberton from Ushuaia, and though they spent most of their time fishing and hunting, some of them engaged in part-time work on the ranch; occasionally as many as twenty were so employed. When the family came to Harberton, Despard and Lucas were fourteen and twelve respectively; but even at that age they could operate a pit-saw for making planks, build a boat and tackle any of the tasks that needed doing.

The off-shore islands were a valuable asset, for sheep and cattle could be kept on most of them without erecting fences, while on Gable Island the need was minimal. The same applied to several peninsulas on the mainland near Harberton which could be blocked across their necks. In this way, by 1894, two thousand acres had been enclosed with only two miles of fence. Hitherto, Gable Island had been inhabited by a large number of foxes which threatened to present shepherding problems; for the Fuegan fox is about three times the size of the English variety; it is in fact more like a small wolf. When, however, some fifteen hundred sheep were released on the Island, a strange thing happened: the foxes were apparently so terrified by this army of noisy invaders that they all swam to the mainland, a distance of two furlongs at the nearest point, and did not return until twelve years later. By that time they had learnt that it was both simple and delightful to kill sheep.

For several years the issue between success and failure hung in a delicate balance, and there were many times when the situation seemed desperate. The long summer days were filled with incessant toil, and though the winter months brought some respite from this because of the short daylight hours, it was replaced by anxiety as the cold and snow took heavy toll of the livestock. During the winter, too, the shortness of the days and the difficulty of moving about through the snow-laden forest sometimes made it necessary for the boys to remain at the place where they were working for months at a stretch, living in wigwams and feeding almost entirely on guanaco meat. It was, of course, the kind of life experienced by most pioneer settlers in the wilderness, but in this mechanical age it is perhaps difficult for us to appreciate all it involved or to understand the deep satisfaction it could offer.

By 1894 the ranch was established as a financially viable proposition. An increasing number of ships which called at Harberton on their way to and from Ushuaia provided an outlet for its produce of meat, wool and timber. The family was able to replenish its supplies and even indulge in some modest luxuries. They were also able to engage some outside help. In 1897, Bridges went to England and returned with a 300-ton brig which he had bought for £900. The following year, while taking a cargo to Buenos Aires, he died. Though this was a terrible blow for his widow, she must have derived solace from the memory of all they had achieved together, and from the fact that he had lived to see his family on the open road to prosperity.

Thomas Bridges incurred a good deal of malicious criticism because he came to Tierra del Fuego as a missionary and stayed there to make his fortune. This indictment, echoes of which can still be heard today, was grossly unjust. No one was more devoted than he to the canoe Indians of the Horn archipelago; no one worked harder or more steadfastly to promote their welfare; no one had so deep an understanding of their complex character and their strange way of life; no one had ever won from them so great a measure of respect and affection. If he were mistaken in supposing that he could improve their lot by inducing them to adopt a more settled way of life, his error was in line with contemporary thought. When he realised that the mission as it was constituted would be powerless to protect the Yahgan from unrestrained contact with the outside world which he was convinced would prove disastrous, he could hardly be blamed for resigning his post. Nor is it surprising that he should wish to remain in the land that had become his only home. It would seem that, in the eyes of his critics, his main transgression lay in the success that attended his courageous venture.

In January 1898, S.S. *Belgica* visited Harberton on her way to the Antarctic. A member of the expedition was Dr. Frederick Cook who was, among other things, an anthropologist. As such, he was greatly interested in the Yahgan dictionary and grammar which Bridges had compiled over a period of more than thirty years. He offered to take it with him and to arrange for its publication in the United States. The author, fearing that his precious work might be lost in the Polar ice, declined to part with it there and then; but he promised to do so if Cook cared to call for it on his way back. Eighteen months later, the expedition, the first ever to winter in the Antarctic, returned to Punta Arenas, whence the Doctor sailed to Harberton in a specially chartered cutter to collect the dictionary. Meanwhile Bridges had died; but the family honoured his promise by handing over the priceless manuscript.

Twelve years later, a party of Scandinavian scientists, also bound for the Antarctic, visited Harberton. From them the family learned that the dictionary was being printed at the Observatoire Royale in Brussels as the work of Dr. Frederic Cook, and that the Belgian Government had contributed 22,000 francs towards the cost of publication. Outraged by this blatant piracy, Lucas Bridges took the first opportunity to go to Brussels, where he had little difficulty in convincing the curator of the Observatoire of the true authorship of the work. No opposition was met from Dr. Cook who, in the meantime, had perpetrated two frauds of a more spectacular nature, which won him temporary fame and lasting notoriety. In 1905 he claimed to have made the first ascent of Mount McKinley, and in 1909 to be the first man to reach the North Pole.

In August 1914, before the dictionary was ready for printing, Brussels and the Observatoire Royale were engulfed by the German invasion; and by the time the war ended, the dictionary had vanished together with the 22,000 francs. However, in September 1929, a member of the Bridges family in England received a letter from Professor Hestermann of the University of Münster, announcing that both the dictionary and the grammar were in his hands, that he was enormously interested in the work and its author and that he wished to know more of both. As a result, Thomas Bridges' youngest daughter, Alice, went to meet the Professor in Münster, and it was arranged that he would prepare the manuscript for publication while her family would meet the cost. A great deal of work was required to translate the author's phonetic alphabet into an accepted system, and the document was still in Hestermann's possession at the outbreak of World War II. By 1945, it seemed improbable that it had survived the saturation bombing of Münster by the Allied Air Forces, and no one was greatly surprised that it had disappeared once again. Luckily, a close friend of the Bridges family, William Barkley, undertook a seemingly hopeless search and, with the help of Sir Leonard Woolley, the distinguished archaeologist, it was eventually found in the kitchen cupboard of a German farmhouse, whence it was taken to the British Museum.

Thus it was that this monumental record of the language of an extinct people, begun by a boy with a dream, compiled in the smoky wigwams of the Horn archipelago, perfected through years of devoted scholarship in the remotest of farmsteads, stolen by a notorious imposter, twice swept away as flotsam on the flood tide of war, found at last a place among the world's most treasured manuscripts.

9 Lucas Bridges and the Ona

THE Ona tribe which inhabited the interior of the main island of Tierra del Fuego and its northern and eastern coasts, differed in almost every respect from the canoe Indians of the channels. Though they killed seals for oil, they were essentially landsmen and did not use boats of any kind. They lived almost entirely on the meat of guanaco which they hunted with bows and arrows, their only weapons. The skins of the animals provided the massive cloaks which covered their bodies down to their ankles and which they discarded when using their bows. They also wore moccasins and Robinson Crusoe hats of the same material. Their shelters consisted of several skins sewn together and placed in an arc so as to form a screen to windward of the fire and sloping slightly towards it. Whereas the average height of the Yahgan men was about five feet two inches, many of the Ona were more than six feet tall and very powerfully built.

The differences between the two tribes were by no means confined to their appearance and their way of life. For example, while among the Yahgan internecine homicide was regarded with disfavour and premeditated murder was rare, with the Ona planned assassination was common. The purpose of these killings was usually to procure the victims' wives, and though they sometimes evoked retaliation, this was not necessarily the case. A captured woman usually acquiesced with complete resignation, though if her new husband treated her too roughly she might try to escape. If caught in the attempt she was liable to receive a severe beating or an arrow through her thigh. Other forms of wifely intransigence incurred either penalty. It may be seen from this that the status of women in the tribe was distinctly subservient, which was certainly not the case among the Yahgan where, though each sex had distinct duties to perform, neither was dominant.

The Ona were divided into three loosely defined groups: one inhabited the comparatively open northern part of the Island; another roamed the heavily forested mountainous area to the south, while a third occupied the eastern peninsula as far as Cape San Diego. There was a great deal of intermarriage between the groups (much of it by force), and each made frequent incursions into the others' territory, often, though by no means always, hostile. Though there was a certain code of group loyalty, there was scarcely any tribal discipline. With no hereditary or elected chiefs, any individual dominance was acquired by physical prowess or cunning. There was also a strong belief in wizardry, and anyone credited with the art could achieve great respect. The perpetual danger of attack put the Ona constantly on their guard, and from this they acquired the habit of moving with the utmost stealth and developed astonishing powers of detection. It may also have been the cause of their reticence which, again, was in marked contrast to the excitability of the Yahgan. Any display of emotion, any boasting or acknowledgement of pain, these were considered unmanly.

All these details about the Ona were discovered by young Lucas Bridges who, in the course of time, came to know them as his father had known the Yahgan and to regard them with admiration and affection. Ever since early childhood he had nursed a longing to explore those unknown ranges which lay so close to his home, and to join the wild people of whom he had heard such fantastic tales from his playmates. For the Yahgan lived in fear of the mysterious race of giants which inhabited the interior, and this was one reason why they never penetrated inland. Presumably these people were the dreadful "Oens men" of whom Jemmy Button had often spoken to FitzRoy. If their devastating raids upon the people of the Beagle Channel were really so frequent as he had claimed, it is strange that not one seems to have occurred after the establishment of the Ushuaia mission in 1869. Jemmy and his friends had also spoken of raids on the islands across the Channel; but as the Ona had no boats of their own it seems unlikely that they would have been sufficiently skilled to handle the delicate bark canoes they may have captured from the Yahgans. Perhaps there was more legend than fact about these stories.

While still at Ushuaia, Thomas Bridges had made two attempts to cross the range to the country beyond where, according to rumour, there was a great lake, as wide and as long as the Beagle Channel. The first had been abandoned because of the fears of his Yahgan companions, and the second was frustrated by bad weather and the difficulty of the terrain. He had hoped to make contact with the elusive Ona; had he done so he would probably have been ambushed and killed without even seeing his assailants. A third attempt had been made by Captain Bové, the leader of the Italian expedition, but also without success. So it was not surprising that Lucas' childhood dream to penetrate the mysterious land across the mountains and meet its strange inhabitants should remain with him through the hard years of adolescence. He had to wait a long time to realise his ambition.

The open pampas in the northern part of Tierra del Fuego, like that on the eastern side of Patagonia, is excellent for sheep raising; and early in the 1890s large areas were leased or sold for that purpose by the Chilean and Argentine governments to companies or individuals. It was of course Ona country, and the presence of these wild nomads posed a major problem in the establishment and running of the farms. Besides their warlike habits, the natives not unnaturally regarded the sheep as a new kind of guanaco, delightfully easy to hunt. Many of the farmers considered that the only solution was the extermination of the tribe and to this end some of them actually employed white hunters who, it is said, were paid about £1 for every native they shot. A more humane, though ultimately no less lethal, method of dealing with the problem was the establishment of two Silesian mission stations, one on the Atlantic coast north of Rio Grande and the other on Dawson Island. Any of the Ona who could be captured or somehow persuaded, were taken to these places to be converted to civilised ways. They did not thrive on the treatment and like the Yahgan, most of them succumbed to diseases hitherto unknown to them.

On the open pampas, the Ona were no match for the white intruders who were mounted and armed with rifles; but in the forested country farther south their superb woodcraft and their age-old skill at concealment gave them such an advantage that no stranger could follow them with impunity. As a result, a natural frontier existed between the opposing forces a few miles south of the Rio Grande, and for the time being the majority of the Ona continued to roam their forests and mountains in complete freedom.

Besides the sheep farmers there was another class of intruder from the north. In 1867 gold had been discovered on the Atlantic coast of Patagonia just to the north of the Magellan Strait. Many years later deposits were also found on the east coast of Tierra del Fuego. Some of the prospectors pursued their quest far to the south and in doing so they came into bloody conflict with the Ona.

During the critical early years at Harberton the Ona did not obtrude, though their sinister presence was keenly felt. In his fascinating book, *The Uttermost Part of the Earth*, Lucas Bridges writes,

"Occasionally we saw, up some distant wooded valley, thin spirals of smoke rising into the clear air; and at times we found places nearer home where Ona hunting parties, or solitary wanderers, had made their fires. There were other signs to tell us that, although we did not catch sight of the Ona, they were nevertheless not far away. Wandering cattle, after being away from the settlement for weeks, would return terror-stricken to the corral and hang around the homestead for days. There were disturbing stories, too, of fatal encounters between the Ona and the mining and farming pioneers who had encroached on their domain in the northern part of the island. It became increasingly evident to us that, sooner or later we ourselves must come to grips with these mysterious, phantom-like people . . . and we hoped our first meeting would not be announced by an arrow in the back while we were cutting timber or walking in the forest. Though we could not enjoy being shadowed, it did not trouble us much. What did concern us were the skirmishes between the Ona and the white invaders . . . those bloody fights with others of our kind were certain, in the long run, to make them number us among their foes."

Nevertheless, late one autumn, when a few days could be spared from the work on the ranch, Lucas persuaded his brothers to join him on a trek into the mountains, hoping to make contact with some of the elusive tribe and to persuade them of their friendly intentions. It was a courageous escapade; but considering that they had lived for many years in close proximity to the Ona without being attacked and remembering that their father's bold tactics in his approach to the Yahgan had always succeeded, it appeared to be justified. After making their way through tangled forest and swamp for ten miles, they reached the foot of what appeared to be the main range. There they found a clearing which had obviously been the site of a large Ona encampment with a dozen fires. Of the people themselves they saw nothing; though, as often before, they had a strong feeling that they were being watched. From there they climbed a ridge to a stretch of bleak moorland above the forest; but before they could gain the crest of the range they met with a blizzard which forced them to return. Fifteen months later, in mid-winter, they tried again some miles west of their previous attempt; this time they were stopped by waist-deep snow. Once again they failed to find the Ona.

To live year after year so close to these shadowy people, to be spied upon and yet to see nothing of them—it was an uncanny situation. In view of what was later discovered about their callous disregard for human life and their ability to attack their prey without exposing themselves to the slightest risk, why did they not kill the brothers when they were out hunting, if only to steal their rifles which they certainly coveted? Could it have been that, just as animals are acutely sensitive to hostility and fear in men, their highly developed instincts made the Ona aware that the white strangers at Harberton bore them no ill will? And when at last they chose to reveal themselves, was it perhaps in the hope of finding an ally?

This occurred in December 1894. Lucas Bridges, then just twenty years old, was living with his two younger sisters in a house several miles east of Harberton, where the main cattle farm was situated. One evening, two tall Indians appeared on the crest of a hill, four hundred yards from the house. Realising that they were Ona, Lucas left his rifle with the girls (aged sixteen and thirteen) and went out to greet the visitors. As he approached, he was relieved to observe that they had placed their bows and quivers on some near-by bushes, evidently to show their peaceful intentions. He decided that it would be better not to invite them to the house lest they should suspect a trick. Instead, he sat down with them and tried to converse. Though they spoke in a harsh, guttural language, of which he could understand no word, their voices were surprisingly gentle and their gestures suggested that they wished to be friends. After a while he intimated by signs that the sun was down and that it was time to sleep. They appeared to grasp his meaning for they rose to their feet, picked up their bows and quivers and departed.

Setting out on horseback the following morning Lucas came upon twenty Ona, including his two friends of the evening before, near the edge of the forest. They received him with dignified courtesy and invited him to sit with them. Presently he noticed that there was an earnest debate in progress and soon it became obvious that he himself was the subject of the discussion. A few years later he learnt the details. Apparently some of the party wanted to take him with them in the hope that, with his knowledge of firearms, he would help them to defend their land from the northern intruders; others argued that the kidnapping would be resented and that it would be a mistake thus to make still more enemies. Evidently the wiser counsel prevailed and in due course Lucas took his leave, not without some feeling of relief. Later that day the whole party came to the house, together with their women and children; then, having been given milk, sugar and biscuits, they went on to Harberton where they stayed for several days before returning to the mountains.

During the year that followed, parties of Ona paid two more brief visits to the ranch. Though they showed no sign of hostility they were very reserved and obviously on their guard. The Bridges family, for their part, were careful to match this restraint and to treat the encounters as casually as possible. Meanwhile they were uncomfortably aware that they were still being shadowed while on their hunting trips in the forest.

In their dealing with the Ona, Lucas and his brothers had the unique advantage of having been born in Tierra del Fuego. From infancy they had played with Yahgan children; they had grown up to regard the natives, not as outlandish savages to be feared, but as fellow human beings with individual characteristics and responsive to friendship; above all they had learnt the art of relaxation when meeting strangers from or in remote parts of the archipelago. Though they found the Ona to be totally different from the Yahgan in their temperament and their manners, they were quick to alter their own pattern of behaviour in sympathy. This patience and tact were rewarded, and it was not long before they were able to break through the barrier of reserve and to establish an easy relationship with their strange northern neighbours. Though their knowledge of Yahgan was no direct help in the difficult problem of communication, it probably made it a great deal easier for them to unravel the complexities of the Ona language and, with diligent application, their ability to speak and understand it grew rapidly.

In 1896 the Ona came to Harberton more and more often and stayed for longer periods. By the end of that year Lucas had begun the practice of going with them on long hunting expeditions, some of which took him into the mountains far beyond the frontier of his previous knowledge. Later he took them by boat to Navarin Island across the Beagle Channel to hunt in country that was entirely new to them. During these excursions, living in close contact with the Ona, sharing their shelter and their food, their successes and their disappointments, he came to know them as individuals and to appreciate the special characteristics of each. He began to acquire an intimate knowledge of their customs, their relationships and their clan loyalties. They spoke quite openly of killing members of rival groups as a recognised method of procuring wives. He soon discovered that, despite their habit of reserve, they had an acute sense of humour; they were fond of playing harmless tricks on one another, which appeared to amuse the victims as much as the jesters. Lucas often found himself the target of these jokes and when he retaliated in kind he met with delighted response. He won further kudos by competing with them in their favourite sport of wrestling; luckily he was powerfully built and was able to give a good account of himself.

News of these friendly dealings with the white people of the Beagle Channel seems to have spread rapidly throughout the widely scattered tribe, and it was not long before members of all three groups were among the visitors to Harberton. While there, as if by mutual consent, they observed a truce, occupying the same camping places, wrestling together, making combined hunting expeditions and sharing the proceeds with every appearance of comradeship and brotherly trust. Once back in their various domains, however, they quickly reverted to their practice of making murderous raids on one another's territory.

Among the regular visitors to Harberton Lucas made many close friends from each of the three groups, and they seemed to become as devoted to him as he to them. In November 1899, he set out with some of them to achieve his ambition to make a journey through the heart of Onaland, across the unexplored interior of the main island to the mouth of the Rio Grande on the Atlantic coast. Through the dense forest the Ona travelled with an effortless gliding movement, following trails that were quite invisible to Lucas and at a relentless pace which they maintained unchecked for many hours together. Thus, in a fraction of the time taken on his previous attempt, they climbed above the forest to the barren moorland beyond, where they had to follow a tortuous route to avoid innumerable basins of bog flanked by craggy ramparts. From the crest of the main divide they looked down a wide valley and over a vast expanse of unbroken forest to a body of water stretching away to the westward. This was the lake, "as wide and as long as the Beagle Channel", of which Lucas had heard vague rumour during his childhood. Known to the Ona as Kami, it was later named Lago Fagnano. He had lived all his twenty-four years on the threshold of this unknown land hidden, so near, beyond the ranges; since childhood he had nursed an aching desire to explore its secrets. Now, seeing it for the first time, he stood entranced while his companions pointed to their familiar landmarks and named the mountains to which ancient tradition had given human personalities and magical powers. Though in the years that followed he became intimately acquainted with this wild country, for him it never lost its charm.

Crossing the range of hills beyond the eastern end of Lake Kami they entered the territory of the northern group. The country there was gently undulating and, though well wooded, it was intersected by many open glades and meandering rivers which flowed northward to the Atlantic. To Lucas it seemed utterly devoid of human habitation, but though they saw no one, the Ona were well aware that their movements were being closely observed, and they remained constantly on their guard until they reached the open pampas beyond the forest.

Lucas' arrival at the Rio Grande with his seven Ona companions created a sensation among the settlers there. It was many years since any white man had attempted to penetrate the forested region to the south, and to do so had long been regarded as suicidal. Now here was this young Englishman who had traversed the entire unexplored area which was known to be infested with murderous savages, and then, after stopping for lunch at one of the farms, calmly started back by the way he had come.

It was soon after this journey that Lucas Bridges began to receive pressing invitations from his Ona friends of all three groups to start a ranch in their territory beyond the mountains. Their motive was fear of further encroachment by the white invaders from the north, from whom they could expect either extermination or internment. They believed that if the Bridges family took over the land they would gain protection from these relentless enemies and retain their freedom. It was a flattering proposition, but though Lucas was deeply touched by the confidence it implied, he was well aware that in the long run there was little hope of stemming the tide of civilisation which must eventually force the Ona to abandon their nomadic way of life. However, he felt that something must be done to help them, and he believed that by opening a ranch as they suggested and by training increasing numbers of them in the arts of animal husbandry he would soften the impact of the inevitable change.

It was a formidable undertaking and, after the years of ceaseless toil that had gone into the establishment of the Harberton ranch, not a little daunting. His brothers were strongly opposed to the plan. They argued that the region was far too difficult of access, that the land they had already offered sufficient scope for expansion without risking their hard-won prosperity on such a hazardous venture, and above all, that the complete unreliability of the Ona and their custom of killing one another would be a source of endless trouble. These objections were doubtless strengthened by the fact that both the brothers were engaged to be married and were thus more inclined to seek security than adventure. At length, after some months of discussion, a compromise was reached whereby Lucas would be free to devote all his time to the new project and if it proved a success the whole family would share the proceeds.

The site chosen for the new farm was an area of comparatively open forest known as Najmishk on the Atlantic coast, well within the territory of the northern Ona. Lucas' first task was to make a track over the mountains by which horses, cattle and sheep could be brought from Harberton. This involved first a careful exploration of the rugged terrain to choose the most favourable line, then the clearing of the way through many miles of dense undergrowth and fallen trees and the construction of timber causeways over innumerable swamps. Though in a direct line it was little more than fifty miles from Harberton to Najmishk, the track itself covered nearly twice that distance. Heavy snowfall brought the work to a standstill during much of the winter and, even with a dozen or more Ona to help him, it was nearly two years before the track was completed. In 1902 he left Harberton with forty-two pack-horses carrying a ton of tools and provisions, and reached Najmishk four days later. He had with him a young Welshman named Dan Prewith, whom his father had brought to Harberton shortly before he died. Together they built a one-roomed hut which they called Viamonte and which was to be their home for the next five years.

It is amazing that they survived, for at that time a state of bitter hostility existed between the northern and the mountain groups; and since their vital line of communication lay across the territory of one while they were living in that of the other, they were at the mercy of both. Two years before, Lucas had had every reason to believe that the perpetual inter-clan warfare was a thing of the past. Moreover he could justly claim to be the principal architect of this change of heart, for he had provided the neutral ground on which all the groups had met and shared the same pursuits and where, to all appearance, they had enjoyed one another's company and established many firm friendships. His hopes were shattered by two particularly brutal massacres perpetrated by the mountain men upon their northern neighbours. What made it especially embarrassing for Lucas was that the instigator of both the killings was a man named Halimink, one of his oldest and closest associates among the Ona. Worse still was the fact that a rifle which he had lent to Halimink was used on the first of the two attacks, which occurred soon after work on the track had started. The second happened while he was on a visit to Harberton from Viamonte.

His lifelong association with the Fuegan tribes made him realise the futility of judging these deeds by his European code of behaviour, or of taking sides in the vendetta which followed. Apart from this it was vital to the success of his project that he should retain the good-will of both parties. Nevertheless, the maintenance of strict neutrality was a delicate and often hazardous task, and despite his care he often incurred the wrath of his friends by fraternising with their enemies.

There were at least two plots to kill him and, considering the Onas' callous attitude to human life, it is strange neither was pressed to a fatal conclusion. Their consumate skill in ambush made armed resistance virtually useless, and his only means of self-defence was that adopted by his father: a bland assumption that no harm was intended and an air of complete nonchalance in the face of threats.

Meanwhile he was tireless in his efforts to persuade his friends in both groups of the utter folly of this internecine skirmishing and that if the tribe were to survive it must cease. Apart from his genuine concern for the welfare of the Ona, for whom, despite their many faults, he had developed a great liking and respect, the success of his venture depended entirely on their mutual co-operation. But it was no easy task by mere argument to change the habit of a lifetime, let alone of many generations.

"For those", he writes, "not acquainted with Tierra del Fuego in those days, it may be difficult to appreciate the degree of nervous tension that, even in times of peace, went to make the mental condition of an Indian, who from childhood had lived the part of hunter and hunted. The intranquility of their minds was betrayed by the care with which they would examine anything that looked like a footprint; by the caution by which they hugged the forest shades and avoided crossing open spaces, where long shadows cast by a low sun might be seen from far away; by the anxiety with which they would notice a flock of birds rising in flight, or a guanaco running as though startled, and speculate on the cause. Much time would be spent lying motionless on some height, intently scanning leagues of forest and the blue distance, searching for the slight variation of tint that would betoken smoke rising from some encampment in the woods. If such should be spied, there would be a serious discussion as to the identity of the wanderers and the reason for their presence there. It seemed second nature, too, that prompted them always to encamp in places affording them a fair chance of escape or defence, in the event of a surprise attack."

Eventually, when Lucas had been living at Viamonte for more than two years, the men of the mountain group agreed to make overtures of friendship. To this end they proposed to revive an ancient ceremony called *Jelj* which bound the participants to refrain from attacking one another. Though only a few of the oldest men could remember having seen it performed, its details were known to everyone. Messages were exchanged and wandering hunters advised so that they could join the group to which they belonged. The site chosen for the gathering was a glade close to Lucas' hut, and on the evening before the appointed day a large concourse of Ona from all three groups assembled in the vicinity. The ceremony began with an hour's complete silence, during which they sat staring at one another across the glade. Then, as though suddenly deciding to take the plunge, the mountain men rose and advanced to the centre where they ostentatiously stacked their bows and quivers. This gesture was followed by a series of speeches in which they asked for friendship and promised to forget their own animosity. Finally there was a curious tournament in which one man after another presented a selected opponent on the opposite side with five blunted arrows with an invitation to shoot at his naked body from a distance of sixty yards while he did his best to dodge the missiles. Deft avoidance and accurate shooting were applauded by the audience with complete impartiality. Despite the blunting of the arrows, when they found their mark they inflicted bloody wounds which were totally ignored by the recipients. On the whole the promises given were faithfully kept, and although occasionally deaths resulted from individual quarrels, there were no more planned raids or fighting between the groups. The long, bloody feud was over at last.

One stormy winter's day in 1907, two exhausted men staggered into the hut (Viamonte), accompanied by an Ona named Chalshoat. They were the first mate and a seaman from the barque *Glen Cairn* which, driven off course by a northeasterly gale, had struck a reef and sunk some distance off shore, near Cape San Pablo. The ship's company, twenty-three men, two women and the Captain's infant son, escaped in two boats. They could just discern the coast through the mist and spray, but a continuous line of huge waves dashing against the rocky shore made it impossible to land. For several hours they struggled at the oars through the heavy sea, keeping as close to the coast as they dared. With nightfall approaching their situation became desperate. Then, through a break in the mist, they saw smoke rising beyond the surf and, steering towards it, they found a place where the waves, though dangerously steep, were not actually breaking. Passing through this narrow gap in the line of reefs, they reached the security of a lagoon beyond.

Alone on the shore waiting to greet them was that notorious assassin, Halimink. He and several other Ona, including Chalshoat, had been camping nearby when they had seen the boats, obviously in distress; so they had lit the fire to guide them to the only gap in the reef. Had the sailors not seen it they would almost certainly have perished. When the boats were seen to be approaching, Halimink had told his companions to hide in the forest lest the castaways should be scared and attempt to put to sea again. As they neared the beach he waded out, carried the infant ashore and then conducted the party to the camp where the Ona gave them food and did all they could to make them comfortable. Twelve years before, near the very same place, Halimink and Chalshoat had taken a leading part in the massacre of six gold prospectors.

By means of signs the Ona managed to intimate that some white men were living somewhere to the westward, and the following morning the second officer and the seaman set out, guided by Chalshoat, to seek help. By the time they reached Viamonte, three days later, the seaman was so exhausted that he could hardly walk. As soon as he heard the news, Lucas collected a troop of horses and, with three young Ona, hastened to the relief of the stranded party. Riding continuously through a night of incessant, driving rain, they covered the distance in fifteen hours.

While preparations were being made to transport the party to Viamonte, it became clear that Halimink had something on his mind. At length he approached Lucas with a conspiratorial air and, referring to the Captain's attractive young wife, said, "The white woman is young and very friendly to us Ona. She is good-natured and always smiles at us. You help the men to get away to their own country, and I will kidnap the woman and keep her in the woods till you return. Why should you live alone?" He was sadly disappointed when, as Lucas put it, "I regretfully declined."

The new ranch prospered. When, after some years of hard and lonely work, Lucas had proved to his own and his brothers' satisfaction that his bold venture was practicable, he went to Buenos Aires where, after prolonged negotiation, he secured the title to 254,000 acres of land. By 1910, "Estancia Viamonte" carried a flock of one hundred thousand sheep, a steam saw-mill had been imported from England and several houses built. In November of that year Mary Bridges, then sixty-eight, travelled from Harberton to Viamonte in a specially constructed sedan chair carried by a team of Ona. The journey took six days. From the pass across the divide she gazed for the last time at the Beagle Channel on whose shores she had lived for nearly forty years. Three years later she returned to England where, in 1922, she died at the age of eighty.

In 1914, Lucas Bridges left Tierra del Fuego to serve in the War. After that, his unquenchable zest for pioneering found outlets, first in the wild and beautiful country between the two ice-caps of Patagonia, and then in Africa, and he only returned on occasional visits to the land of his birth.

For many years it seemed that his fervent desire to ensure the welfare of the Ona would be fulfilled. As the Viamonte ranch developed, more and more of them were employed in such tasks as shepherding, shearing, fencing and breaking horses, at which, in time, they became very competent. For the most part this employment was seasonal which suited the Ona admirably for it meant that they could return frequently to their hunting grounds and thus satisfy their strong nomadic instincts. In time, however, many of them drifted into the towns which had sprung up in the northern part of the island and in this alien world they quickly degenerated. Even so, with the kind of encouragement and understanding that Lucas Bridges had afforded, the tribe might have survived had it not been for two epidemics of measles which, brought from the towns, swept through the land in 1924 and 1929, and in which seventy-five per cent of them died. From this disaster the Ona never recovered, and within a few decades that splendid race had ceased to exist.

Today Estancias Harberton and Viamonte are managed by the grandchildren and great-grandchildren of Thomas Bridges. Countless travellers have enjoyed their generous hospitality.

10 "Ancón sin Salida"

RETURNING from our expedition to the Cordillera Darwin in March, 1962, Cedomir and I decided to spend a fortnight in an attempt to investigate Mount Burney. Our time was limited by my companion's obligation to return to his job at the University in Santiago at the end of the long summer vacation; but we thought that with luck it might be enough to learn something about this curious mountain.

Mount Burney is supposed to be an active volcano; if so it is the most southerly in South America and very far indeed from its nearest neighbour. I had tried to discover something about it, but a search through several geographical libraries and consultations with some leading authorities on the distribution of volcanic activity had yielded a very lean harvest of information. Perhaps more remarkable was the fact that Cedomir, an adventurous young geologist who had spent most of his adolescence living in Punta Arenas, knew no more than I. The mountain had been seen and its outline sketched by Lieutenant Skyring during his first passage of Smyth Channel in H.M.S. *Adelaide*. Indeed it was probably he that named it, since Admiral Burney (who had sailed with Captain Cook) was then a senior member of the Board of Admiralty. In 1910 it was reported by a ship's captain to be in a state of violent eruption. Apart from its geographical position, that was about all we could learn. Yet nowadays it is frequently seen—as indeed it has been for nearly a century—from ships passing through Smyth and Union Channels on their way from Punta Arenas to Valparaiso and to Puerto Natales.

This universal ignorance about a familiar landmark is not uncommon in the Land of Magellan where even today the frontier of knowledge is often the boundary of the most distant sheep estancia. The farmer has enough to do coping with his own wide acres to bother with the untamed and perhaps uninhabitable country beyond. On the other side, once a shipping route had been found through the vast jig-saw of islands comprising the southern coast of Chile, there was little incentive to penetrate the innumerable side-

157

channels or to explore the inhospitable land surrounding them. In time, no doubt, population pressures and other developments will change this situation. Until comparatively modern times it was by no means unusual to live on the edge of the unknown; today, in other parts of the world, it is rare indeed.

Mount Burney stands near the northwest corner of a block of land of about 2,000 square miles known as the Muños Gamero Peninsula, which is almost completely surrounded by sea water. Indeed it is only connected to the mainland by two tiny necks of land, collectively known as the *Paso del Indio* because the nomadic Alakaluf Indians occasionally carry their canoes across them from Obstruction Sound to Skyring Water. It was this very isthmus which had foiled Skyring's ambition to find an alternative passage to the Strait of Magellan.

The easiest way of reaching our objective would have been to persuade the captain of a northward bound ship to drop us off at the northern end of Smyth Channel and to pick us up on his way back. No doubt, too, the Chilean Navy would have agreed to provide the necessary transport. But both these plans would have taken far too long to arrange. The alternative was to approach the mountain from Skyring Water. It promised to be an interesting journey; for, so far as we knew, no one had ever visited the interior of the Muños Gamero Peninsula, let alone crossed it. It had, however, been roughly surveyed from air photographs, and the map showed that much of it was occupied by a system of inter-connected lakes which extended from the *Paso del Indio* to a point some twelve miles south of Mount Burney. Luckily we had with us the *Zodiac*, the inflatable craft which we had used to reach the Cordillera Darwin; for no boat could have been procured locally that was both robust enough to withstand the storms we were likely to meet and light enough to carry across the *Paso*.

As we needed a third man, Cedomir persuaded a young cousin of his, Ricardo, to join us; and early in the morning of March 12 we set out from Punta Arenas in an army lorry. The road to Puerto Natales, after crossing a stretch of open pampas, follows the eastern shore of Otway Water, close to the place where *Beagle*'s boat crews so narrowly escaped disaster, and thence along FitzRoy Channel. A few miles beyond this extraordinary river-like passage, which was teeming with black-necked swans, we turned off the main road and ran westward for another twenty miles to Estancia Skyring on the north coast of Skyring Water, where we were welcomed by the owner, Mr. Friedli. As it was the last ranch in that direction the road ended, and we had intended to proceed from there in the *Zodiac*.

When he heard of our plans, our host showed great concern and tried to persuade us to abandon them. For Skyring Water is a very large sound, eighty miles long, completely exposed to the prevailing westerly gales and, like all the channels in that part of the world, subject to sudden violent storms. To him, it seemed madness to venture on it in a small inflatable boat. However, when we explained that the *Zodiac* was a replica of the craft in which Dr. Bombard had crossed the Atlantic, and that I had already used it extensively in Patagonia, he was prepared to believe that we knew what we were about. Our main problem was petrol, for we could not carry more than 40 gallons. We estimated that to reach the end of the unknown lake system would involve a voyage of 180 miles there and back. To make any headway against a powerful wind and a heavy sea it would be necessary to run the motor at full throttle which would consume fuel at a very high rate. Unless we were exceptionally lucky with the weather on the outward journey our only chance was to keep close inshore using whatever shelter we could find from headlands and bays. Unfortunately, 25 miles beyond the estancia, the long, mountainous peninsula of Cerro Castillo stretched from the north coast half way across the Sound. To get round this would not only involve a long detour but would expose us for many hours to the full force of the wind. However, the base of the peninsula was connected to the mainland by a low-lying isthmus, little more than a mile wide, and Mr. Friedli kindly offered to send a *peón* with three pack horses to meet us at that point and to transport our boat and supplies across it.

He also told us that, although there was no road, it was possible to take the lorry along a forest track to a bay ten miles farther along the coast. After giving us an excellent lunch in his beautifully appointed house he sent us on our way with his young son to point out the trail. This last courtesy was scarcely necessary for, grinding along in bottom gear, we went so slowly that the *peón* with the horses had no difficulty in keeping ahead of us. It was late afternoon before we reached the bay, beyond which further progress in the lorry was barred by marshland. An hour later we launched the *Zodiac*, heavily laden with petrol drums, and set out on our voyage.

As soon as we left the shelter of the bay we met a strong headwind and a boisterous sea. The waves dashed over us and before long we were soaking wet, very cold and devoutly thankful that we were not destined to punch our way round the peninsula. Dusk was gathering when we rounded a headland and saw a log cabin standing above a sheltered bay where we had arranged to meet the horses the following day. It was the last permanent habitation on the northern shore of Skyring Water, and its owner, Danial Lever, lived there alone, tending a few sheep and cattle, and tilling a small plot of land. Obviously delighted by our unexpected arrival, he greeted us with great enthusiasm as we landed and conducted us to his home. There we lost no time in stripping off our sodden clothes to stand naked before a roaring stove, while he set about the preparation of a large stew.

We had been told that Danial knew more than anyone else about the western reaches of Skyring Water; but though he was a compulsive talker—a product, no doubt, of his loneliness—it was hard to steer the outflow into fruitful channels. At length it transpired that even his knowledge was very vague. The *Paso del Indio* was little more than a name to him; he had never been there and had no idea what it was like; and he assured us that no one except the Alakaluf Indians had ever crossed it. He told us, however, that on one of the many islands beyond the peninsula, there was a log cabin used intermittently by a family who made a living by cutting cypress and transporting the timber during the comparatively calm winter season to a sawmill at the eastern end of the Sound.

I had begun the day with a slight fever, and now, having been thoroughly chilled, I felt far from well. So after supper I took my sleeping bag to the second room of the cabin and lay on the floor, thankful now to escape the oppressive heat of the stove. A restless night left me feeling much worse and I decided to spend the day in bed. At noon the *peón* arrived with the three pack horses and Cedomir, Ricardo and Danial set off with them to transport the *Zodiac*, the motor, the petrol and food across the isthmus, an operation which required two relays. It was a filthy day and I lay listening to the wind howling through the forest outside and the rain lashing the walls of the cabin.

Night was falling when the party returned, wet and tired. They had crossed the isthmus with the first batch of loads, but on the way back one of the horses had plunged into a bog. They had spent some hours trying to extricate the wretched animal without success, and at length they had had to leave it so as to reach the cabin before dark. The next morning Danial produced two horses of his own and we set out with the remainder of our baggage distributed among four beasts.

Though my fever had left me I was still feeling light-headed as we made our way along the shore to the isthmus. It was still blowing hard, but the rain had stopped and some shafts of sunlight pierced the ragged clouds racing overhead. A section of the forest had been burnt to make room for grazing land, and the white skeletons of the trees thronged like a multitude of ghosts around the bay. Beyond stood the rugged mountains of the peninsula which still held patches of snow that had survived the summer. Finding a route across the isthmus which avoided the swamp we reached the farther shore by mid-afternoon. Though we offered to return with Danial and the *peón* to help with the rescue of the unfortunate horse, they made it clear that they would prefer to manage alone. Later, we heard that they had succeeded by towing the creature to safety with the other four horses harnessed to a long rope.

Having inflated the *Zodiac*, we used our small mountain tent to construct a cabin which would accommodate one of us at a time, keep our bedding dry and minimize the shipment of water. Against a stiff on-shore breeze we had difficulty in launching the heavily laden boat through the breakers and starting the motor before we were blown back to the beach. Our fifth attempt was successful. We were now in a land-locked gulf at the base of the peninsula and, in spite of the wind, the waves were small. Unfortunately, after we had been going an hour the motor began to give trouble and we could not take full advantage of the favourable conditions. At 6.30 we passed through a narrow strait forming the entrance to the gulf, and soon afterwards we landed on a small beach, enclosed by thick forest, with a stream of sweet water near by. Many fresh tracks and fresh droppings showed that the place was frequented by wild cattle; and Cedomir, who had had some alarming encounters with these animals, insisted on building a strong stockade around our camp. However we were not disturbed.

We had hoped to reach the *Paso del Indio* the following day, but we spent the whole morning and much of the afternoon tinkering with the motor, and by the time we had corrected the fault only a few hours of daylight remained. It was particularly irritating because the weather was unusually fine and calm. At 7.30, as dusk was falling, we reached a large island and ran into a small cove on its eastern shore where, happily, there was fresh water. There we found an old Alakaluf encampment: the remains of a fire and a circle of withered saplings which had formed the framework of their wigwam. Two rocky headlands enclosed the bay, which was fringed with tall trees and flowering shrubs crowding so close to the deep, clear water that there was no beach. It was a lovely evening, so still that even the sea beyond the cove, silvered by the light of a crescent moon, was velvet smooth.

The next morning, March 16, we awoke to a fiery dawn, magnificent and menacing. But though the long streamers of crimson cloud across the sky threatened a return of bad weather, it was still perfectly calm when we left the cove at 7.30. Half an hour later we passed close to an island where we saw the cabin belonging to the wood-cutter whom Danial had mentioned. To seize the advantage of the calm weather we cruised at full speed and by 10 o'clock we were approaching the northwest corner of Skyring Water. Here there was a sudden change of scene. Hitherto we had been on a wide expanse of water, broken by a few large islands and surrounded by mountains, sombre and remote. Now we were in a maze of channels divided by innumerable mossy islets, intensely green, and small, craggy promontories overhung by twisted trees; a miniature, intimate landscape, like a Chinese painting.

Our problem now was to discover the way across the isthmus— the southern part of the legendary *Paso*—separating Skyring Water from the lakes of the Muños Gamero Peninsula. We had expected to find a strip of flat land, possibly a shallow river valley draining the lakes; but a careful search revealed no such place. At length we reached a circular lagoon at the extremity of the northernmost channel and moored the boat in a creek overhung with massive fuschia bushes and other flowering shrubs. From there we went forward to reconnoitre, each taking a separate line. After scrambling over several wooded hills, I reached a point from which I saw a fjord stretching away to the northwest—obviously part of the lake system we sought. But though the southern end looked close, I could see no easy way of reaching it. Returning to the boat, however, I found that Cedomir had discovered a practical route, though he warned us to be prepared for some heavy work.

It was then 1 o'clock. Rain was falling steadily, and though the water in the lagoon was unruffled, broken cloud racing low overhead told a different story. Before tackling the portage we made a cache of petrol and food for the return journey, which we buried deep in the undergrowth against the chance of some Alakaluf passing that way. These canoe Indians are the counterpart of the Yahgans who used to inhabit the Fuegan channels. They, too, have been tragically decimated during the last half century, and although they were not yet extinct, it had been estimated that there were not many more than one hundred left. As these were distributed along many hundreds of miles of the Pacific coast it was highly improbable that any would come to that place during the next two weeks. Moreover we were far from sure that we had found their *Paso*.

The crossing of the isthmus involved, first a steep slippery ascent through dense bush, then a stretch of open swamp followed by a climb to a col and finally an abrupt descent through forest to the shore of the lake. The most awkward item to be transported was the *Zodiac*. The hull without the floorboards was wrapped into a bundle weighing 150 pounds and strapped to a frame which we each carried in turn. Though the total distance was little more than half a mile, it took us five and a half hours to carry everything over, and it was almost dark before we had finished the job, which resulted in a miserable, makeshift camp. In the dark and the pouring rain I could produce nothing better in the way of a fire than a smouldering, smoky heap; so we stripped off our wet clothes, squeezed into our ill-pitched two-man tent and slept till dawn.

The drab scene was then transformed. The rain had stopped and the air was still. The cloud covering the sky and the hilltops was salmon pink. The forest trees—nothofagus, cypress and magnolia—in various shades of green, the banks of emerald moss lining the shores, the clusters of red flowering shrubs completed an extravaganza of colour which, in absolute silence, was mirrored on the smooth surface of the fjord. From the resinous wood of a dead cypress trunk we built a large fire and hung our clothes to dry while we ate a leisurely breakfast and assembled the boat. It was 9 o'clock before we continued on our way.

Presently the fjord opened into a wide lake, dotted with islets. To the east there was a stretch of flat land which must have been the second isthmus connecting the Muños Gamero Peninsula with the mainland; beyond it lay the lagoon at the end of Obstruction Sound where Skyring's hopes had been shattered. In most respects our surroundings were similar to those we had seen the previous day in the northwestern corner of Skyring Water, and they had the same magical quality. But there were some differences. As we had expected the water of the lakes was fresh; because of this and because there was no tide, the dense, moss-covered thickets crowded even closer to the water's edge, with the result that some of the islets resembled floating satin pincushions. There was, too, a notable lack of bird life. On Skyring Water we had seen large numbers of wildfowl, black-necked swans, steamer ducks and cormorants; here there were none.

Though by now dark bands of cloud were moving swiftly southward across the sky, the air about was strangely calm. In every quarter, both near and far, showers of rain were interspersed with shafts of sunlight, a combination which produced the most amazing display of rainbows I have ever seen—complete arches, double bows and broad, opaque pillars of brilliant colour, some so close that we seemed to be in their very midst.

After steering a northerly course for ten miles we entered a narrow channel running westward between steep banks of forest broken occasionally by foaming cascades and waterfalls. Then and later, I felt a sense of loneliness stronger than I have experienced in any other part of Patagonia or Tierra del Fuego. For all its haunting beauty, there was an atmosphere of hostility about this land, as though it resented our intrusion. Perhaps it was just a trick of the rapidly changing light, or perhaps the absence of life amid such luxuriance; maybe it was because I was too acutely aware of our reliance on our boat. Certainly it would be difficult to escape without it; and the country, for all its soft blandishments, would not be kind to castaways. It was hard to believe that here, among these unknown lakes, we were still within seventy miles of a farmstead equipped with every modern comfort.

By noon we were approaching the western end of the channel opening into the largest of the lakes stretching twenty miles from north to south. The size of the waves warned us that we were about to meet a strong northerly wind, but we were not prepared for the vicious squall which struck us as we rounded the point. I was about to turn back to the shelter of the channel when I saw a snug little bay with a beach just round the corner. I opened the throttle and drove towards it, cutting the point so fine that we were nearly driven on to a reef. For this clumsy piece of seamanship I received a gentle rebuke from Cedomir. Two hours later the weather moderated and, though there was still a strong northerly wind and a heavy sea, we started on the last stage of the voyage. Even with the motor running at full speed we made slow progress, but matters improved as we approached the northern end of the lake which we reached at 6 o'clock, two hours before dark. Running the boat up a long creek between tall reeds, we found a pleasant camp site in a grove of trees.

The following morning we reviewed our situation. It was now March 18, six days since we had started. The voyage had taken much longer than we had expected. We still had ten days' food left and a further three days' supply had been dumped at the Paso. Mount Burney was now about twelve miles away to the northwest, but unless the terrain should prove much easier than we had reason to expect, it would take us all of a week to cover that distance and return. This would leave six days' food for the voyage back which, with a following wind should be much quicker. But food was not the problem. Ricardo, who had taken a fortnight's leave from his job, and Cedomir were expected back in Punta Arenas on March 26 and it now seemed as though we might be nearly a week late. Only a short time before we had caused a great deal of unnecessary concern when, in both the Chilean and British press, we had been reported missing in the Cordillera Darwin, due to our failure to make radio contact with the naval station on Dawson Island, and we did not relish the prospect of a repetition of that situation. So it was with some misgivings that we decided to press on to Mount Burney with a week's food.

To the north our view was blocked by a steep mountain, partly covered with snow. Two thousand feet up, beyond the tree-line, a broad terrace appeared to extend round the unseen western face and to offer a good route at least for the first two miles. To reach it we had a long and exhausting struggle through a dense entanglement of dwarf nothofagus. When, with some excitement, we rounded the corner of the terrace, we found ourselves looking down a sheer precipice to another large lake, which seemed to curve round the northern side of the mountain. While contemplating this unexpected sight, we were smitten by a sudden hurricane from the northwest and everything was obscured by driving sleet. It was almost impossible to advance against the wind and we sheltered behind a boulder until it became apparent that this was no mere squall. Then, though nearly three hours of daylight still remained, we stumbled back round the corner to find a place to pitch our small bivouac tent.

When, in the early hours, the wind died away and the rain ceased it became very cold, and by morning our clothes, soaked the evening before, were stiff with frost. Moving rapidly to get warm we climbed diagonally up the mountain and in an hour we reached a northern shoulder of the summit ridge. Already the sun was shining; and, gradually, as the surrounding mist dissolved, a wide view opened before us. Astonished, we saw yet another lake lying at the eastern foot of our mountain, its far end hidden behind the distant ranges in that direction. Northward we looked across a vast green plain to a silver strip which must surely be Sarmiento's *Ancón sin Salida* leading to Skyring's Kirk Narrow. It seemed strange indeed, after nearly four hundred years, to be making fresh discoveries within sight of that historic landmark.

A distant cloud to the northwest was slow to depart, but eventually it vanished like the rest to reveal the great bulk of Mount Burney. Instead of the simple volcanic cone I had been expecting, it appeared as a broken massif of peaks and ridges, heavily glaciated, and dominated by a sharp white fang. We were already fairly certain that we would not be able to reach it, and we decided to go forward without our loads to make the most of the fine weather.

The northern side of the mountain descended gently towards the plain in a series of wide, concave terraces filled with woods and tarns and meadows. Enclosed by high cliffs, each was a little world of its own, as green and warm and fragrant as a Devon coomb on a summer's day. At length we reached the edge of a precipitous slope dropping seven hundred feet to a deep channel which connected the two lakes and separated the mountain from the green plain. This formed a decisive barrier to our further progress and as it would have taken far too long to return to the boat and carry it through the forest to either of the great lakes flanking the mountain, we had no choice but to abandon our project.

Neither Cedomir nor I felt any disappointment. The journey thus far had been so rewarding and the discoveries of that morning had provided such a splendid climax that there was no room for regret. Basking in the sun on a grassy ledge and gazing out over the wonderful panorama of mountains and lakes, we discussed plans for returning to this exciting place. We agreed that we would need at least a month to make even a cursory exploration of Mount Burney and the surrounding country.* It remained an intriguing enigma. None of the other mountains appeared to be of volcanic origin, though Cedomir was convinced that the green plain had been formed by immense deposits of volcanic ash blocking a fjord which had once connected the lakes with the sea and had probably bisected the Muños Gamero Peninsula. On the terraces we found scattered deposits of pumice, apparently of fairly recent origin, which had obviously been blown there by the prevailing northwesterly winds.

Twenty-four hours and one storm later, we were back at the creek where we had left the *Zodiac*. While I cooked a meal and added to my collection of *collembola*, my companions cut a young cypress and with this, a climbing rope and the tent, they rigged a sail to speed our return voyage. At 3.30 we set off down the creek. The sail proved most effective, and as soon as we were beyond the shelter of the forest we stopped the motor and ran before a stiff northerly

* The following summer, before starting on my second expedition to Tierra del Fuego, I carried out this project with John Earle and Jack Ewer.

breeze, steering with two oars. On entering the east-west channel, however, we lost the wind and had to continue with the motor.

The rain had held off since noon and the wind had not been excessive, but when, soon after 6.30, we reached the lake of the pincushion islets there was a sinister light which could not be explained by gathering dusk. We had intended to camp near the exit of the channel, but it was clear that we were in for a major storm and we decided to press on while conditions were still reasonable. With the petrol saved earlier we could afford to run the motor at full speed and, helped by the sail, sped along at more than six knots. Even so it was eight o'clock and almost dark by the time we reached the fjord at the end of the lake, and we had scarcely scrambled ashore when the storm broke. In torrential rain we stowed the boat and pitched the tent; but it was too dark to make much of a job of it and once again in this place we had to put up with a makeshift camp. At least we were sheltered from the wind which, judging by the noise it made, must have been very heavy.

Crossing the isthmus took us all the next morning. Except for a few showers the rain had ceased, but the wind was evidently set for a prolonged blow. When the baggage had been carried to the far side and the *Zodiac* assembled and loaded, we sat for a while beside a large fire and ate a leisurely meal. We were in no hurry to face the storm and considered postponing the ordeal until the following day; but on the principle that it never pays to wait for Patagonian weather, we decided to resist the temptation, and at three o'clock we started.

The narrow channels leading from the *Paso* were calm, but as soon as we reached the open water beyond we met the full force of the north wind and a heavy sea. It had been our intention to steer southeast across a wide stretch of open water direct to the end of the Cerro Castillo peninsula; but the waves looked so intimidating that we ran for the shelter of the islands we had passed on the outward journey. In doing so we had the wind abeam; but the *Zodiac*, now less heavily laden, was as buoyant as a cork and only an occasional wave broke over the side. Even so, plenty of water was shipped in the frequent squalls of spindrift, which kept us busy bailing.

Soon after six we reached the island of the woodcutter's cabin. We were not sorry to get ashore and the prospect of shelter was more than welcome; for by then it was raining hard and the force of the wind was increasing. The cabin itself was locked, but we found lodging in a shed which, though dilapidated, had four stout walls and a roof. It contained a varied collection of objects—old clothing, otter skins and strings of dried mussels. There was also an ample supply of firewood and a stove made of a rusty oil-drum with a length of piping for a chimney. It was not long before it was red hot, and we sat naked, sweating as though in a Sauna bath, while our clothes steamed on a climbing rope slung overhead.

Another unwonted luxury was a cabbage which we had found growing near the cabin and which made a welcome addition to our evening stew. The shed was inhabited by a colony of cats who resented our intrusion, but became more hospitable when they found what we had to offer. From their scraggy appearance it was evident that they found life on the island hard to sustain. As the fury of the storm continued to mount, we became still more aware of our good fortune in having found such a snug billet, though we expected soon to be deprived of our roof; but, though it leaked, it clung on manfully. The noise of the wind and rain were so loud that we had to shout to make ourselves heard. Nevertheless we slept for eleven hours.

When we awoke, though it had stopped raining, the wind was as strong as ever. There was no question of putting to sea in these conditions and we settled to the agreeable prospect of an idle day. After breakfast I climbed to the top of a hill which commanded a view over the island. It was a remarkable sight. The sea was white with flying spume which hid the lower part of a neighbouring island, half a mile away, while the channel between looked like a cataract. At 2 o'clock, however, a definite slackening of the wind and a brighter sky suggested that the worst of the storm was over, and we decided to leave. We paid for our night's lodging—and the cabbage —by leaving a supply of tea and sugar in the shed.

It was not long before we realised that we had been deceived by a temporary lull, for we had scarcely reached the open water beyond the islands when the wind, shifting to the northwest, regained most of its former ferocity. We were now steering S.S.E. for Punta Laura at the extremity of the peninsula. With the wind on our starboard quarter we were making a great deal of leeway, so we had to keep far out from the coast to avoid being driven ashore. We might have sought refuge in one of the bays on the coast of the peninsula, but it would have been a hazardous operation in such weather. Moreover, in the face of a northwesterly gale, which could persist for weeks, it might be hard to escape. With a reasonable amount of ballast, the *Zodiac* is almost impossible to capsize, and it will remain buoyant even when completely filled with water. Our only cause for anxiety was lest the motor should cease to function, a disaster which would leave us helpless.

It was an exhilarating run. As though on a surf-board, we would ride the crest of a breaking wave then, overshooting it, the boat would plunge into the deep trough beyond, bouncing like a rubber ball, while the spindrift flew overhead. I scarcely noticed that I was soaked and numb with cold. To port the cloud-capped mountains loomed above us; to starboard we saw nothing but the storm-tossed sea. By six o'clock we were racing past the tall escarpment of Punta Laura, its very summit lashed by spray, and soon afterwards we found refuge in a wooded bay beyond the cape. It was a pleasant spot, completely sheltered from the wind and with banks of fuschia in full bloom lining the rocky shore. Its only defect as a camp site was lack of water, but eventually we found a stagnant pool in the forest, and although it was the colour of tea, it tasted sweet.

It was blowing as hard as ever the next morning. Before leaving, I climbed the escarpment to enjoy in comfort the splendid spectacle of the storm beating against the point and to relish the smug satisfaction of having weathered it. By hugging the east coast of the peninsula we kept in comparatively calm water, and soon after noon reached Danial's cabin where we received an enthusiastic welcome. There was another visitor who turned out to be the cypress merchant, our unwitting host of two days before. He and Danial plied us with questions about our journey into the unknown country beyond the *Paso del Indio*.

After lunch we set out on the last leg of the voyage. We were soon beyond the shelter of the peninsula, but as the wind was astern there was no risk in keeping close inshore and with our improvised sail and the motor running at full speed we skimmed over the waves like a steamer duck. Half way along the coast there was a sandy spit running far out to sea and separated by a narrow strait from Isla Juan. The strait was marked on our map, but as the island overlapped the spit on its western side it was invisible until we were within fifty yards of the shore. The water beyond presented a curious sight: though it was quite calm it was white with spume. The final hazard was a reef of barely submerged rocks off the last headland. We gave it a wide berth and shortly before 7 o'clock on March 23 we ran the *Zodiac* on to the beach at Estancia Skyring. Stiff with cold we made our way to the house where we were cherished with all the luxuries that one could expect to find in an affluent English home.

But for the motive of reaching Mount Burney we would not have attempted to penetrate the Muños Gamero Peninsula. Though failing to achieve our objective, we had been richly rewarded. In a journey of less than twelve days we had seen a new aspect of this wild, lovely land, and enjoyed a generous share of its sweets. Incredible though it seemed in mid-twentieth century, we had actually extended the discoveries of Sarmiento and Skyring. I had certainly gained a clearer insight into the hazards faced by those old explorers in their open boats, and a deeper admiration for their achievements.

Index

171

Last Hope Inlet

Rio Gal

Disappointment
Bay

Canal of the Mountains

Kirke
Narrow

Easter
Bay

Sound

②
Mount
Burney
MUÑOS GAMERO
PENINSULA

Obstruction

Est. Skyring

Beagle
Hills

Oazy Harbour

2nd Narrows

Skyring Water

Fitzroy Passage

Smyth Channel

Punta
Laura

Elizabeth
Island

ape Pillar (Desire)

S T R A I T

Mercy
Bay

Tamar Bay

Desolation

Island

Otway Water

Punta Arenas

M A G E L L A N

B R U N S W I C K

Jerome Ch.

P E N I N S U L A

④ Port
Famine

① Port Gallant

SANTA INES
ISLAND

Gayetano

Ch.

S T R A I T

I.

Cape
Froward

O F

Dawson
Island

Adi.

Clarence
Island

M A G E L L A N

Magdalen Channel

Gabriel Channel

Monte
Sarmiento

C O R D I L L

Fury Bay

Breaknock

Peninsula

London
Island

Whaleboat

Sound

Cape Desolation

York Minster

March H

P A C I F I C

O C E A N